IS LEADERSHIP MALE?

IS
LEADERSHIP
MALE?

by

Joan Martin

NELSON WORD PUBLISHING

IS LEADERSHIP MALE?

ISBN: 1-86024-304-5

Reproduced, printed and bound in Great Britain for Nelson Word Ltd.

96 97 98 99/10 9 8 7 6 5 4 3 2 1

Acknowledgements

My thanks are again due to my husband Daryl for his patience in making the necessary editorial and grammatical corrections within this book, and to those of my children still at home—Jonathan, Mandy, Ruth, Sheila and Clare—who have given me their help to enable me to finish this sequel to *The Ladies Aren't For Silence*.

My thanks are also due to Christine Noble for her great Foreword and to Elaine Storkey for her challenging Conclusion. Both ladies are extremely busy, and I am very grateful for the time they have given. Thanks too to Angela and Sharon for their excellent typing.

Finally, very many thanks to every gentleman in this book who has entrusted me with his words. I trust that the spirit of what has been communicated is true and that people will take sufficient encouragement from what has been shared to begin to see real active change happening within the communities of their churches. I thank God for living at this time and being a part of this restoration.

Contents

Foreword

WE LIVE IN A TIME OF great change. The map of today's world looks very different to the map of just a few years ago. Some people are struggling into a fresh expression of nationhood, from a position of apparently silent aquiescence. The most bloody and prolonged situation has to be the former Yugoslavia a troublespot well exposed to the media. They do not, however, stand alone. We, as well as the newsreaders on TV, are having to get our tongues around fresh names, and our minds around fresh boundaries in the atlas. Another example is in Germany, where the Berlin wall has fallen and Germany is once again one nation. Worldwide we have witnessed ongoing birth pangs in order to bring to birth something new. This is also true of the Church of Jesus Christ in these closing years of the twentieth century.

The Body of Christ worldwide is experiencing an intense outpouring of the Holy Spirit. As a result people's lives have been radically changed, and in many Churches there is a new fervour for God's word, God's holiness and God's commission at all levels. There are ongoing struggles, however, which no-one in their right mind can possibly deny. The words of Isaiah 43 v18-19, leap from the page in a fresh way, almost as though they are in a bolder print than before. 'Forget the former things, do not dwell on the past. See I am doing a new thing! Now it springs up, do you not perceive it? I am making streams in the wasteland.'

Perhaps not so very long ago, we would have answered this question by saying, 'Yes Lord we do see what you are doing.' Today many of us, however, are now saying, 'No Lord we are not so sure that we do see it, but we trust you for the new shape and any changes you may want to bring about.' God in fact answers His own question. What He wants to do is always the same. 'I am making streams in the wasteland.' His heart has always been to make the desert bloom.

It may sem shocking to suggest this, but one of the desert places in our churches is to be found amongst women. They suffer from such low self-esteem. They fear criticism. They struggle as to what they may or may not do. They are confused by God's apparent blessing in areas of their lives that appear at times to be in conflict with the teaching of their leaders. One of the questions which needs to be answered is this—is leadership male?

The ongoing struggle for greater understanding of the role and purpose of women is linked to the ongoing love that the Lord has for the whole human race. This book documents the anwers of some male leaders in the church to the relevant questions in this subject. In some denominations and streams, the questions have already been answered to their satisfaction, and they are moving forward with their particular understanding and flavour. For many others there is a continuing struggle going on. Joan Martin has sought to reflect some of these views, and I trust the book will make interesting, enlightening and challenging reading.

Let me leave you with some words from Eugene Peterson's *The Message*. This is the last paragraph from Romans 11.

Is there anyone who can explain God?
Anyone smart enough to tell Him what
    to do?
Anyone who has done Him such a huge favour
    that God has to ask his advice?
Everything comes from Him!
Everything happens through Him!
Everything ends up in Him.
Always glory! Always praise!
Yes. Yes. Yes.

Christine Noble

Introduction

THE ISSUE OF MALE and female is the oldest issue in the world. Countless words have been both spoken and written, so why bother writing another book on this subject? We have had both secular and theological exposition, demonstrations and even legislation, yet the issue remains one that does not go away.

The Church lags behind the world in having few female leaders. Yet a quick scan of history shows that it is not just feminism which brings this issue to the fore today. In pre-history women had position and recognition. In biblical history this was also true. Deborah, Priscilla and Phoebe, to name a few, were women of note. It was not until the Council of Laodicea in A.D. 363 that the office of female elder was abandoned according to Dorothy Pope in her book *God and Women* (IVP).

In church history both male and female leaders were persecuted. The Anabaptists, Quakers and Methodists all had women leaders, as did the Salvation Army as early as 1875. Many women were leading missionary societies by the end of the last century, and the Suffragette movement was born at a similar time. All this predates feminism.

More recently from 1987 to 1992 half those who became ministers in the church were women, according to Marc Europe's report of 1992–93. According to their information, the Bapist Church has accepted women as probationary ministers since 1922, while the Methodists have been ordaining women since 1972. Within the Salvation Army 60 per cent of officers are women, whereas in the Afro-Caribbean Churches 39 per cent of ministers are women. In 1990 there were no female ministers in the FIEC Churches and only 16 per cent of Congregational ministers were women.

In England, further figures reveal that only one Anglican minister in twenty is a woman, yet in Protestant churches 56 per cent of their missionaries are women! Even in the Roman Catholic church, which does not ordain women, more than half of its missionary workers are women. The relatively new House Church movement, however, at this time had no female ministers!

Within recent cultures femininity has been condemned for a season, as in the time of the cultural revolution in China in the 1960s under Chairman Mao. Yet sons of women know that there is a difference between the genders and look at it at times with fear and at other times with awe. My own son Jonathan sat behind me as a toddler to look for the eyes in the back of Mummy's head! The mysterious difference has never been totally fathomed and yet the unknown remains a threat.

Since the subject has already been treated from the women's perspective it seems only fair not to let the gentlemen be silent, but rather to let a dozen of them already in leadership, answer questions frankly concerning their attitudes towards women, with particular reference to women in leadership in the church. In asking these questions I have aimed to provoke good answers, which will facilitate men and women working together for the kingdom of God. Since I wrote *The Ladies Aren't for Silence*, the issue of women in leadership in the church has remained ever present, and will continue to be so until women with gift are in places of recognised leadership.

In interviewing the gentlemen, I used eighteen questions which form the basis of the eighteen main chapters of this book. Most of the denominations already mentioned are represented by the men I have interviewed for this book. It is, therefore, with pleasure that I commend these gentlemen to you, as they seek to be frank concerning their thoughts and feelings. I trust that their commitment to see women functioning is being outworked more and more amongst them in their local churches. I thank them for the privilege of being trusted to relay as faithfully as possible the heart of the matter, as they see it. Their responses will illuminate the way ahead in the near future in their own churches and I trust in many others.

The Questions

Ted Dobson in *Healing the tear in the Masculine Soul*, says that a male defines himself by what he does, for example, his work, sport, politics, social action, or by who he knows or what he owns. Leanne Payne in *Crisis in Masculinity*, says that true masculinity is the power to honour truth, to speak it and be it.

Question One

What do you regard as describing true masculinity as distinct from femininity? How are men and women different and how are they the same?

In the introduction to *Crisis in Masculinity*, Leanne Payne says that a mother cannot finally tell her son that he is a man...and that in adolescence we are all listening for the masculine voice, to give us pictures in our hearts of who we are as people in our own right.

Question Two
How did you find your own masculine identity and security?

C. S. Lewis writes in *That Hideous Strength* that 'the male you could have escaped, for it exists only in the biological level. But the masculine none of us can escape. What is above and beyond all things is so masculine that we are all feminine in relation to it.'

Question Three
Are you aware of the other side of your personality which has feminine traits? Have you, for example, developed your intuition?

SECTION TWO
MEN IN RELATIONSHIP TO THEIR FAILURES.

Michael Korda in *Male Chauvinism* says that the male chauvinist is not the proud figure that men take him to be, insisting on his legitimate superiority over women, but rather a man who cannot accept the responsibility for the failures of his life and therefore assigns them to women.

Question Four
How have you personally overcome chauvinism and the potentially destructive use of male power?
Dave Tomlinson in *The Ladies Aren't For Silence*

says that the notion that women should not teach because of Eve's deception is preposterous.

Question Five

Do you believe women are more easily deceived than men? What is your personal experience of male deception?

Gordon Dalbey in *Healing the Masculine Soul* talks about the 'feminisation' of the Church in almost all denominations. Leonard Le Sourd in *Strong Men, Weak Men*, talks about men allowing women to dominate in the Church by their own absence and silence.

Question Six

Was passivity ever a problem in your life? If so, how did you overcome it to function in life and ministry?

SECTION THREE
MEN IN RELATIONSHIP TO THE CHURCH.

Gordon Dalbey in *Healing the Masculine Soul* says that in our Western culture there is no validation of manhood.

Question Seven

How do you facilitate secure men in the Church today, with clear life goals and ministries?

Karl Stern in *Flight from Women*, in his chapter on

the philosopher Goethe, quotes him as saying, that the spirit of unbridled activism of insatiable curiosity and conquest needs womanhood, the holy passivity of the 'be it done unto me', as its complement.

Question Eight

How have you overcome male chauvinism in the Church? Have male passivity and male deception been issues that you have had to deal with?

David Pawson in *Leadership is Male* says that 'Patriarchal society is a reflection of divine fatherhood.'

Question Nine

Does the Bible teach patriarchy in the Church?

SECTION FOUR
MEN IN RELATIONSHIP TO WOMEN.

Quotes are often made such as 'an English-man's home is his castle,' 'women need to submit,' and 'leadership is male.'

Question Ten

As a man today, how has the cultural atmosphere of insecurity and fear of women affected your views of authority and submission? Are women in any way inferior to men? What do you feel that God originally intended for Adam and Eve?

Karl Stern in *Flight From Women*, says that men 'murder' their mothers in their aggression towards their wives!

Question Eleven

Has your relationship with your mother (or father for that matter) affected your subsequent relationships with women? Are you aware of having been controlled by such relationships and then later determining not to allow a woman to control you again?

Kierkegaard the philosopher talked of the terror of commitment and said that for there to be a real love commitment, death must occur in the lover!

Question Twelve

How has your attitude to your wife, if you are married, affected your attitude to women in general and women in leadership in particular? If you are not married are you aware of any link?

SECTION FIVE
MEN IN RELATIONSHIP TO WOMEN IN THE CHURCH

It has been said elsewhere that God intended a covenant society, but Israel became a society of the ruled and the ruler. One aspect of this was men ruling women. Tony Campolo in *20 Hot Potatoes Christians are Afraid to Touch*, writes that evangelical Christianity in general has evidenced a hypocritical duplicity by sending women to be preachers in difficult situations overseas, while denying them the right to be ministers at home in the US.

Question Thirteen

Do you as a male leader assume authority or do you feel women are emotionally equipped to handle authority and rule?

Christine Noble in *The Ladies aren't For Silence* talks in terms of two orders. One is the social order for families and the other is the church order for people with gifts and ministries for the Church.

Question Fourteen

Do you differentiate between the two orders, social and church? Are there differences for women in the roles they play and is gender related headship in the home the same as or different to gender-related leadership in the Church? Are there in fact leadership gifts to executive level in both sexes?

In Ephesians 5:21, all believers are to be subject to one another. Gilbert Bilezikian in *Beyond Sex*

Roles points out that only equals can be subject to each other. No officer can subject himself to his men and while a junior officer obeys a senior, only one soldier of equal rank with another can willingly choose to submit to him.

Question Fifteen
In Church order do you see a gender-related hierarchy or do you look for a mutuality amongst men and women leaders, within the context of team work, where the Holy Spirit is Lord?

SECTION SIX
MEN AND WOMEN TOGETHER FOR THE KINGDOM

Mary Stewart van Leeuwen in *Gender and Grace* says that the chief New Testament metaphors for being Christian are concerned with the female, for example new birth, nurturing, caring, being a servant, and becoming as a little child. She feels that Christian men have handled such conflicts by turning the Church into a hierarchical institution, to distance themselves from their 'feminisation' as Christians and from women fellow believers.

Question Fixteen
How can we in the Church change men's thinking in order to facilitate change, to see men relinquish overall control and to see women emerge into

leadership in mutuality with men, as part of the team?

John Stott in *Issues Facing Christians* today says, 'I conclude with some central simplicities. If God endows women with spiritual gifts (which he does) and thereby calls them to exercise their gifts for the common good (which he does) then the Church must recognise God's gifts and calling, must make appropriate spheres of service available to women, and should ordain (that is commission and authorise) them to exercise their God-given ministry at least in team situations. Our Christian doctrines of creation and redemption tell us that God wants his gifted people to be fulfilled, not frustrated.'

Question Seventeen
How can we in the Church change practices to facilitate change to see women in leadership in mutuality with men as part of the team? How do you facilitate women with leadership gifts into leadership in your church?

A well-known international speaker at a large Christian conference in England said that there was male apartheid in the Church. He stated that many men in the Church had voted for Margaret Thatcher to lead Britain, but they would not allow her to speak in their church!

Question Eighteen

Today in the 'outworkings' of church, there is generally no Jew nor Greek, and no slave nor free, but this is not so for male and female. Do you foresee a day, in church life, when we will begin to take back the ground of joint rule that Adam and Eve lost to the enemy?

Who's Who

DAVID ALTON

David was born in the East End of London. His mother was Irish speaking, and his father a Cockney and a manual car worker. Whilst a student in Liverpool, he was unresolved over whether he should be an overseas missionary or go into teaching. He taught for two years in Kirby and for five years with children who had special needs.

At 21 he was elected to Liverpool City Council as councillor for an inner city area, which he has represented ever since. In 1979 he was elected as youngest member of Parliament for a seat in Liverpool. He has continued to represent them and enjoyed an increased majority in 1992.

David is married with three children. He is co-founder of the Movement for Christian Democracy, an interdenominational group. He is also Parliamentary sponsor of the Jubilee Campaign and a trustee of the charity Crisis at Christmas, the largest charity working with homeless people. He has written three books.

DAVE BILBROUGH

Dave was born in Hackney in East London in 1955. His parents were not Christians, although he now has one sister, who is a Christian. He came from a musical family and became a Christian at the age of seventeen. He finally became a musician after he was converted. Through the work of a local youth group in a Baptist church, Dave found God and four years later he was baptised in the Spirit. In the mid-seventies he met Pat, they were married in 1978, and have two children, Jonathan who is twelve and Daniel who is ten.

Dave is regarded as one of the most established songwriters and worship leaders in Britain today. As well as leading celebration events throughout Britain, he has also toured in the United States, various European and Scandinavian countries, the Far East and Ghana. From listening to the questioning songs of Bob Dylan and Paul Simon, Dave has found answers to those questions in Jesus and seeks to share his faith through his music. He is now a member of the Pioneer Team, which works mostly into new churches at home and abroad.

STEVE CHALKE

Steve was born in South London and went to a local Baptist church which, finding boring, he eventually left. Having fallen in love with a girl, he started going with her to the church Saturday night youth club. They then started attending church on Sunday evenings and Steve became a Christian at the age of 14 in a coffee bar called Impact. He knew that if Christianity was the truth he had to give his whole life to it.

As a teenager Steve had a vision and knew, for example, that he would be working with the homeless in cities. A lot of what is now happening at the Oasis Trust is an outworking of this teenage vision. God told him that in working for the poor, he was to start a hostel, a school and a hospital. The first hostel for the homeless was opened a few years ago. The school is still in the planning stage. The hospital for the homeless, which everyone said was impossible, has now opened—the Elizabeth Baxter Health Centre. The building was donated and £200,000 was raised to fit it out. It fits in with all the government legislation and offers a unique service providing primary health care in liaison with several central London hospitals.

Steve is now the National Director of Oasis Trust, and the Christmas Cracker initiative. There are over 100 people working in and out of inner London from the Centre. He is becoming a well-known television presenter and is married to Cornelia and has four children.

GERALD COATES

Gerald was born in Woking, Surrey on 25th November 1944, and has lived in or near Cobham all his life. He was converted at Coombe Bassett near Salisbury in Wiltshire in a summer youth camp in 1956 when he was eleven.

He was nominally Anglican and later in his late teens went to a Plymouth Brethren assembly. He was baptised in the Spirit whilst riding a bicycle and was then asked to leave the Brethren church. He started Cobham Christian Fellowship (now called Pioneer People) which was one of the first house churches, and are now called the new churches. He married Anona in March 1967. They have three children, Paul, Simon and Jonathan.

Pioneer People, with its 'church-plants' now involves 1,200 people. Gerald's main responsibilites are with the Pioneer Team, and a network of 60 churches involving almost 10,000 people. Pioneer also runs a number of evangelistic training courses, most of which are over subscribed. In partnership with others Pioneer has helped launch the March for Jesus, Pioneer for AIDS (now ACET), Romania Aid and the Jubilee Campaign. and has started a number of overseas churches and initiatives in South America, Norway, Sweden, Eastern and Western Europe and Africa. Its work is explained and updated through a quarterly magazine.

At present the work is centred on London, in prayer, evangelisation, church planting, social action and working with other churches such as Kensington Temple, the Ichthus network, and Holy Trinity Brompton. Gerald wants to be instrumental in bridge building and envisioning in order to see the nation networked with the Gospel and appears from time to time on television and radio.

JOEL EDWARDS

Joel was born the last of six children in Kingston, Jamaica, West Indies. He left in 1960 when eight years old and came to London. He became a Christian at the age of eleven. When he was twenty he went to the London Bible College after which he married Carol.

For a short while he worked as an ancillary probation officer and then did further study in social work. On becoming qualified, he was employed as a probation officer in London for about 10 years.

He began pastoral work in 1985 in the East End of London. When he left the probation service, he began working as a General Secretary of the then West Indian Evangelical Alliance of which Philip Mohabir is the chairman and founder. The Alliance is now known as the African Caribbean Alliance. Within the EA, Joel has become the UK Director.

Joel and Carol have two children, Joel and

Davina. They live in Leyton and are based in the New Testament Church of God, which has a pastoral team of three ministers, with Joel as the senior pastor. The church is part of an international Pentecostal body, which began in about 1886 in the United States of America. It came out of Methodism and the holiness movement and took on the Pentecostal mantle in 1906. Functioning in 110 countries world-wide it now has millions of members. In the UK, there are 110 churches with a membership of 8,000 and adherents of 15,000.

ROGER FORSTER

Born in 1933, Roger trained at St John's College, Cambridge from 1951 to 54. He was converted in 1951 and was baptised in the Spirit in 1953 at Cambridge, where he graduated in mathematics and theology. From 1957-74 he was an itinerant evangelist and in 1974 he founded Ichthus Christian Fellowship, which he has led ever since.

The Ichthus Christian Fellowship is located in inner London and made up of a church fellowship of twenty-nine congregations (including some overseas) and many training programmes and social action projects. (Ichthus is a Greek word signifying Jesus Christ, Son of God, Saviour.)

Roger has evangelised and taught the scriptures in many parts of the world, has run a home for people with social problems, has worked in evangelism in places ranging from universities to the back streets of London, and now ministers at many churches and church conferences all round the world.

Among his many responsibilities, Roger is one of the founders and directors of March for Jesus, one of Tear Fund's honorary vice presidents, and he is on the international board of the AD2000 Movement and the council of the Evangelical Missionary Alliance. Roger has written six books, which include *God's Strategy in Human History* and *Reason and Faith*.

In 1965 he married Faith, who also has a vital ministry in Christ and a story of her own to tell. They have three children and one grandson.

TONY HIGTON

Tony was born in south-east Derbyshire. Both his parents were Christians and attended a small mission. He was converted at the age of 8. As a teenager he went to a Christian Brethren Assembly and at the same time was assistant superintendent of a Methodist Sunday School. He was baptised at 13 years of age in the Brethren Assembly and eventually went to the London Bible College in 1962. There he met Patricia who initiated him into the mysteries of the Church of England, and he liked what he saw.

Both Tony and Patricia had independently thought that they would be going abroad to work as missionaries. It later became clear that God had not called them to do this, and Tony began to think about being ordained into the Anglican ministry, even before becoming an Anglican. As things became clear, he was confirmed and then spent two years training at Oak Hill College. Afterwards he became curate at Christ Church, Newark in Not-tinghamshire. After Christ Church they spent a further five years in Cheltenham, before coming to Essex in 1975, where they still work. Their ministry today is both local, national and international.

Patricia and Tony were married during his training in 1966, the afternoon that England won the World Cup! They have two married children.

R. T. KENDALL

Robert Tilman Kendall is an American from Kentucky, but he has now lived in England for 18 years, with his wife Louise, who was from Illinois. He was converted at six and a half years of age on Easter morning in 1942. Feeling convicted of his sins, he told his father that he wanted to be a Christian. He prayed with his parents and asked God to forgive his sins. The family attended the Church of the Nazarene.

On completing school he went first to Toevecca

Nazarene College in Nashville, Tennessee, where he got his B.A., and afterwards he married Louise. He then went to the Southern Baptist Seminary in Kentucky where he got his MD, in Theology. Later, he went to the University of Louisville and gained an MA, before going on to Oxford University to study for a doctorate of philosophy.

Robert Tillman Kendall came to lead as pastor at Westminister Chapel in 1988, five years after Martin Lloyd Jones had retired. He has two children Tillman Robert and Melissa.

PHIL MOHABIR

Phil Mohabir's grandparents were from India. In the 1880s British agents came recruiting young men and women to become labourers on their sugar plantations in the West Indies and Guyana. Phil's grandfather was promised gold if he emigrated from Gorkhpour. He went never to return and died a broken man.

Phil was raised practising the Hindu religion. While attending High School in Georgetown, British Guyana, he was asked to read part of Mark's gospel. Doing so, he became aware of a presence in the classroom and felt as though Jesus was there gazing down at him. He heard a gentle loving voice say 'Follow Me'. He struggled for three months before deciding to follow Jesus.

Later Phil felt the missionary call to England.

He arrived in 1956 and God led him to work with various groups and eventually to live in Brixton, London. There, in 1958, he was married to Muriel who is of Jamaican descent. They have six children. Through his many links Phil was enabled to bring the West Indian Evangelical Alliance now known as the African and Caribbean Evangelical Alliance to birth in England. He has continued to work and minister in the Guyanas, the West Indies, Sweden and England, whilst living in Brixton.

JOHN NOBLE

John was born into a family with strong Salvation Army roots on both sides. His father died when he was just sixteen and his mother found it difficult to control him as he was already running away from God. He became increasingly caught up in a wild life of parties and drinking which often involved the occult, particularly the ouija board. This activity escalated after he joined the Irish Guards for National Service. The pay was low and with nothing to do in the winter evenings they turned to seances. He became known as the 'Ghost Man' after giving some scaringly accurate predictions.

During his time in the army he met Christine whose family were Eastenders and who consistently dabbled in spiritism, fortune telling and the like. They went deeper together into trances, poltergeists, automatic writing and visions. Having met with a personal devil John became open to the supernatural element of Jesus' ministry and began to search for God. He worked in an Oxford Street fashion store when Michael Harper, a young curate at All Souls, Langham Place, became chaplain to the store. They met and Michael was a great help, also with a Baptist couple who befriended them locally. Within months of coming back to God, and Christine deciding for Jesus, they were baptised in the Holy Spirit and delivered from occult activity at a mini revival in London.

He soon found himself ministering around local churches and set up a series of meetings in Ilford during 1961 entitled 'The Work of the Holy Spirit in the Church Today'. They were packed with folks from all church backgrounds. Soon he and Christine opened their home to those who were being saved, healed and filled with the Holy Spirit. They really thought they were one of the only groups of this kind in the country.

However, through contacts with such men as Arthur Wallis, Peter Lyne and Graham Perrins, they quickly discovered that God was raising up networks of 'new churches' all over the country. Arthur Wallis called a group of seven men together for fellowship and dialogue, and from this gathering apostolic teams emerged, working here in the UK and overseas. For some years John lead one such team of over thirty men and women drawn from churches within their care until his friend Gerald Coates received prophetic words to the effect that they should linkup ministries together. John has consequently had involvement with 'Pioneer' for the last five years.

DAVE TOMLINSON

Dave was born in Liverpool. At the age of four, his father became a cripple for the rest of his life. He had thought he would never marry, but met Dave's mother in the waiting room of a hospital. The elders of his church were opposed to his marriage, telling him he had no right to get married because he would not have children and would not be able to care for a family. The net result was that he remained a devout Christian all his life but never went to church again.

Dave was sent to church from an early age, and recognises now the effect these events had on his life. His mother assumed the strong role of provider. Economically things were hard, whilst the Brethren Assembly Dave attended was full of fairly wealthy people. Being on the fringe and dissatisfied with life, at the age of seventeen he read *The Cross and the Switch-blade*. This set him looking for the experience of being baptised in the Spirit. He eventually found this in a church in Liverpool which also stressed holiness.

Dave married Pat and after living in Ripon and Middlesborough they eventually moved down to London to work particularly with young people in the Brixton area. Dave now feels they are recovering things which were to be found in the early house church movement in an alternative way. For Dave and Pat their home is a major tool in this work. 'Teamwork' was closed after twelve years, because the model of an apostolic work was not one Dave was happy with any longer. He now feels called to reach not the unchurched but the unchurchable and is more comfortable in the prophetic role, which this requires.

CHARLES WHITEHEAD

Charles was born in Cheshire in 1942. His father was away serving in the army and he did not see him until he was about three years old. During the war the family lived with grandparents. Charles' mother was a Roman Catholic and his father a nominal Anglican, who later began to worship in the Roman Catholic church. Charles was brought up a Roman Catholic, attending the local Catholic school.

At eleven he transferred to a Roman Catholic boarding school. Whilst there Charles learnt a great deal about faith and Christianity and when he left he felt he was a committed Christian. At university he found that his Christianity did not really work and whilst reading American history, which was the shortest course that he could find, he gave up his faith altogether. He married Sue, who was in a similar spiritual position.

Ten years later they came back to faith through the witness of christian friends in their locality. Persuaded against their will to go along to a faith sharing group they encountered a very real living faith listening to people's testimonies and reading the scriptures. Sue gave her life to the Lord and was baptised in the Spirit. Shortly afterwards Charles also found God, while visiting St. Andrew's, Chorleywood and listening to Barry Kissell who, although a stranger to him, asked Charles if he knew that God loved him and that God wanted to change his life. He took him aside and prayed for him. The next day the presence of God came upon Charles while he was sitting in a church and, being moved to repentance, he was baptised in the Spirit.

Charles and Sue had been brought back to faith by a combination of Catholics, Anglicans and Baptists and they decided to worship locally, going to each other's churches. Charles is still fully committed to the Roman Catholic church and Sue is committed to the Anglican church. Because the people who brought them back to faith were linked into what is now called the charismatic renewal, they also felt very much a part of that. They started to attend a local Friday night meeting of

Christians from many churches, a group of thirty to forty which still meet in their house (20 years later). In their Roman Catholic church fifty people out of 2,000 would be recognised as charismatic. Within the church as a whole, however, there would be many more whose faith had been brought alive as a result of those fifty people.

Charles is a member of the National Service Committee, which facilitates renewal in the Catholic church by putting on conferences and teaching programmes. Internationally, he is president of the International Council for the Renewal in the Roman Catholic church. Twenty people meet twice a year to talk about what is happening around the world and support one another. The more affluent Western Christians provide the material resources to help in Africa and Asia.

Charles still works part time for a Swedish forestry company. The rest of his time he works for the renewal of the church. It grew rapidly in North America and Europe in the 1970s, whereas in Africa, Asia and Latin America the growth has been much greater in the 1980s. It is thought that there are around eighty million nominal Catholics worldwide who have been renewed in their faith, and most of these people, who would be recognised as charismatics have gone back into normal church life re-equipped in grace and new life, rather than remaining closely identified to the charismatic renewal.

MEN IN RELATIONHIP TO THEMSELVES

CHAPTER ONE

True Masculinity

WHAT IS MASCULINITY and femininity? What characteristics make the difference between a man and a woman? Is there a normative base line in all our male and female characteristics that, within life in general and the Church in particular, would make life relationships easier to understand? To answer these questions fully we need to consider what the Bible has to say about male and female, how individuals relate and something of the different cultures of the world. That task is awesome. Another approach is to ask some of the leading men in church today both nationally and internationally, to answer certain questions from their own understanding, life and experience.

This issue is riddled with controversy. Maleness is biological, yet Simone de Beauvoir said many years ago that, 'The body and biology is not enough to define woman!' Masculinity is said to be about the value which men (rightly or wrongly) place upon themselves, but women have had a part to play in birthing and raising all male children as well as female! Culture therefore must have a bearing.

Roger Forster begins for us by agreeing that men often do find their value and identity in their work. He continues, 'Serious theologians say that ultimate value is found in our relationship with God, being outworked through our being and what we are in ourselves.' Leanne Payne's statement that true masculinity is the power to honour truth, speak it and be it, is true as long as it is understood that the pursuit of finding out what is ultimate and identifying with it is 'honouring truth, speaking it and being it'. This is our only value, whether male or female.

'The particular temptation of the male is to abandon identifying with and being the truth. He rather finds his value in what he can accomplish. Yet there are thousands of males worldwide throughout history, some starving to death in prison, who have never found their value in work.

'Building self-worth on what you do is very insecure. Integrity means that we speak the truth, if we believe in what we have found to be true. Generally we then want to share it with other people, whether we be man or woman.

'I therefore prefer to think in terms of masculinity and femininity rather than male and female. The female has marginally more of the feminine in her and she is actually able to think on her feet, and while speaking. The male tendency is to think through, by retreating into the reflective. One is not better than the other—they are just the two parts of our make up and both are necessary to express truth. My wife Faith often speaks whilst feeling her way towards the answer, whereas I do not want to say anything until I have got an answer, and we both want to express it when we have reached out conclusions!

'Biblically there is very little difference between male and female. The only difference the bible confirms is that biologically a female gestates, lactates and menstruates. Other distinctions tend to be the dominance of the masculine over the feminine. The masculine impregnates and is often the initiator emphasising work, but the calling of the Lord is that we discipline that which is easy to us, to compensate for that which is not so predominant. The Lord did this all His life and we all need to seek to gain that balance. The woman's role of receptivity, which can have a bad tendency of passivity, also needs to be compensated. A man needs to develop the gentle side, hence the concept of 'gentleman', with its consideration for the other when doing his activism. The woman, however, needs to stir herself from her passivity and become a courageous sister!'

Joel Edwards sees men and women alike in terms of their spiritual being, made in the likeness and image of God. He sees no superiority nor inferiority in that, only differences. He explains, 'Thinking about masculinity, I have to ask first if it is something of a sociological structure within each culture, as distinct from manhood and maleness, which is created biologically by definition. I feel the need to talk not so much about masculinity but rather maleness, as complementary to womanliness. There is a very definite created complementary intention, which we must explore and pursue, apart from sociological structures.'

Charles Whitehead is not sure that he agrees with Leanne Payne's definition of masculinity, because he does not see why the power to honour truth, to speak it and be it should be any different for men than it should be for women. He continues, 'These things describe any person of character rather than masculine or feminine people. I grew up without my father until I was four, although my grandfather was around. In those early years, as a result of seeing him as the man who was the provider and who set standards in the home, I thought of the man in the family as the authority figure.

'At the end of the war, when my father left the army and returned home, these ideas were reinforced. However, for myself, in the teenage years I moved towards seeing this issue much more in terms of equality. I went through a change of mind and redefined masculinity and femininity much more in terms of character than anything else.'

Tony Higton found this a difficult question to answer, because he feels that masculinity and femininity can be rigidly defined in categories. He explains, 'In many ways we are talking about differences of degree, and whatever is said there will be exceptions. I see masculinity in terms of being more of an initiator, whereas femininity has more the essence of a responder. Out of context, this can sound like a 'put down' for women, but there is truth in it, in spite of the exceptions. Males tend towards domination, whereas women tend towards nurture. Men are more concerned with things, whereas women are more concerned with people.'

Dave Tomlinson feels this question is a good one to answer, having come from a position of having clear answers some years ago, yet now feeling he has less clear answers than ever. 'Having described how God created male and female, with their physiological differences, the Bible does not then go on to give prescriptive roles of masculinity and femininity. The sociological view is also unhelpful, because people come with their own preconceived agenda, much of which is unconvincing.

'We cannot be adamant as to how much is learned and how much is inherent. Although I describe myself as a feminist, one of my reservations about feminism is that it tends to lose that part of humanity which we describe as femininity. In general terms men do tend to be more aggressive and women more nurturing and both are important aspects of humanity. In my relationship with my wife, my male aggression is not my preserve alone. However, as we are all learning, sometimes one does feel threatened.'

The issue of threat and fear is a key one in our attitudes towards masculinity and femininity. It has caused tension throughout the ages. To move from fear to freedom, masculinity, whether macho or meek and its consequent feminine response must be faced and understood not just biologically but also as culturally learned, if acceptable, and with the need to relearn if culturally unacceptable. Prayer, training and counselling may be needed for the Christian.

Steve Chalke talks of the media image of masculinity as one where the man has the right shape of body and never cries! Yet he finds attributes of true masculinity in women. He explains, 'Going through a whole list of masculine attributes and qualities, I could not find anything that I feel should be the exclusive role of a man as opposed to a woman. God created both man and woman in His own image, both capable of at best reflecting His character and at worst falling far short.

'I used to have a friend who did a lot of very intricate crochet, and I immaturely thought there was something wrong with him. That was my conditioning concerning what a boy could or could not do, yet what he was doing was actually very creative and, therefore, reflected God. When a man and a woman buy a house they both see it as good, but they will be seeing it from different perspectives. She might see the detail of the fireplace surround, he the size of the room. In partnership, the masculine and feminine complement each other.'

David Alton sees the lines between men and women as very blurred. He feels we sometimes spend too long exaggerating the differences, rather than looking for the things that unite humanity. 'I fully understand why some women feel society has treated them badly and that some male attitudes and domination certainly need to be questioned. I also feel that an over-reaction can lead to a diminution in the role of men, and a stridency and extremism which will not do women any favours.

'All people are different, each one is unique and we are bound together in communities. It is fascinating to see in my small children the characteristics developing in them that clearly define them as very different from each other. We have a girl aged five and two boys aged three and one and a half, and without any encouragement from us one is clearly predominantly feminine and the others masculine. Each one must be prized as being unique regardless of their sexuality.'

R. T. Kendall recognises that God in creation made man and woman differently. 'For a man to be masculine means that he is not effeminate. What has been missing in man in recent years is a rugged maleness. Men seem to be getting more feminine and women more masculine, which I see as role reversal. I do not agree with people who say that there is little difference between male and female, because I think that there are many differences.'

Gerald Coates agrees with Ted Dobson that men find their masculinity in what they do in terms of sports, politics, social action, work and in their possessions. 'The power to honour truth, to speak it and be it, however, is not just masculinity, but rather true humanity and personhood for any human being, whether male or female.

'I see the difference between men and women as small. Issues of character such as being honest, sensitive, submitting to one another are all fruits of the Spirit and the Spirit does not have distinctly masculine or feminine traits. All in the Body of Christ require these fruits.

'It is true to say, however, that women tend to be a lot more intuitive than men. This is not necessarily how it should be, but is perhaps a more cultural issue. Women can be expected to develop home-making abilities and care for children, where intuitive abilities are developed. Men, however, who are in business in a logical world, often deal in papers, models and diagrams.'

John Noble concludes on this question, without wishing to stereotype the sexes. 'Once the stifling pressure of male dominance has been removed and over-reaction to its consequences dealt with, more and more people seem to be accepting that the old concepts of what is masculine and what is feminine are not so way out. Women appear to be generally intuitive and protective, feeling things far more intensely than men. They tend to be romantic as opposed to being sentimental, which is often a male trait. Men are frequently clinical in their approach and more competitive, and a man needs to be understood, whereas a woman needs to be loved. At worst our differences can be seen as weaknesses, obstacles to be overcome or enemies to be conquered. If this is the case, we re-enact the "battle of the sexes".

'True masculinity will face responsibility squarely and contend fearlessly for truth and justice. True femininity will stand alongside with the encouragement and support of insights and understanding. To say roles could never be reverse in men and women is folly, for we are not talking about physical and sexual differences which are to be honoured and preserved in this life.

'God has not divided masculinity and femininity into two watertight compartments. There is something of each gender in both men and women. Sadly, in view of a man's desire to escape his duties and a woman's overriding sense of responsibility, we tend to try and find peace and fulfilment in the classical male–female roles. This is not necessarily wrong. However, the key to success is finding security in what God has made us to be, whilst refusing to allow Satan to put us beyond the edge of our own unique individuality into a perversion of it. If we discover the strength of our diversity, we can stand together as a full expression of the image of God. I believe this diversity can co-exist in leadership structures as well as family life.'

So in conclusion we see clearly that if the Church is to reach men, as it can and must, then the issue of masculinity needs to be addressed. We are all to be loving, thinking and creative people in relationship to one another. Men are not the norm with women the deviants from the norm, nor are men and women just a created biology with subsequent biological roles.

The general attitude abroad is often that manhood must be achieved at all costs, whether by that society means sexual initiation, starting work or some other form of aggressive action. These things do not in themselves make the distinction between boyhood and manhood. Traditionally masculinity has depended on physical strength and aggression, yet Jesus was vulnerable. Today we expect men to be controlled powerful human beings, yet Jesus wept. A women arrives at womanhood, but culture takes men into manhood, albeit in a confused way. We in the West lack initiation in this area, whilst other cultures often have great initiation ceremonies. In some measure the Church must facilitate its families, who often struggle with a muddled world. It must sound a clear clarion call that the Christian man is to be as attractive as Jesus, a man of character, strong and yet vulnerable, each one with God's unique gifts.

CHAPTER TWO

Personal Security

MANY MEN FEEL THEY are still on the road of discovery in finding out about their masculinity. They find it as other men provide role models, and through working alongside men who affirm them. Some men who do not love sport, for example, can be looked on as inferior, yet they may excel at art, music and creativity. Other men who truly want the best for their wives may fail as husbands, through their inability to communicate and function effectively.

In the cut and thrust of this issue another issue looms large. Culture can play an important part. In some cultures men give more than they take. They are nurturing and generous. In other cultures they can be controlling. So masculinity is to some extent outside the man and yet has great bearing on how he lives. How men learn to be men ultimately affects how they relate to the women around them. Masculine identity is, therefore, a vital part of our discussion.

David Alton says that he does not feel that anyone ever entirely finds their own identity. The searching goes on. He continues, 'The deeper you move into your faith, the more you feel that your understanding is too shallow. For me, from my days as a student to my being elected a city councillor, doing something to help people has given me a sense of responsibility and security. However, when my daughter was born and she was very ill, visiting her brought deep emotions that I did not know I possessed. I had worked with children with special needs for five years, yet this event shook my security.

'People influence people. I have two or three mentors now and just as Jesus provides a blueprint for living life, these others have also had an input into my life. This must include parents with my mothers constant and committed faith that has been passed on to me.'

R. T. Kendall, who was raised in the United States of America, makes a very simple statement. 'I did not go looking for a masculine identity, because I did not have a problem about my own masculinity.'

Others have found personal difficulties that have affected their lives. **Joel Edwards,** who spent some of his childhood in Jamaica and some in England, explains, 'Being without a father after the age of eight meant I had little appreciation of having a "real man" about the house. My older brother became a hero for me, although I never grew up with him in the way that I grew up with my sisters. As a teenager I realised I was bereft and looked to the church for answers. I developed with much trial and error from the simple issue of shaving through to becoming a father myself.'

Tony Higton, being a sickly child who was over-protected, also looked up to a brother who was eight years older than him. He explains, 'He was athletic and adventurous, whereas my father, although a believer, was a very fearful man. I picked up this fear particularly his fear of emotions, and was extremely shy until my teenage years. In my mid-teens I determined to break out of this, in spite of being quite insecure. I played rugby and went on "outward bound" courses and my insecurity became internalised for many years.

'In all this, there was great emotional cost for me in terms of fear, some of which was irrational, but God enabled me to obey Him quite radically in the ordained ministry in spite of the fears. I was eventually helped through prayer counselling. I wanted to be free from fear, and the counsellors prayed for me. I then had a strange experience. It was as if I sat watching myself resist their prayers, which was not what I wanted. It was only after a prayer of deliverance from fear that I sensed a great release.

'A few years later the Lord called me to a wider ministry and I found myself confronting the denial of biblical truth within the Church of England and taking on the establishment. My main fears had been of bishops clamping down on me or of receiving negative letters. This time was also part of the healing process and I would not have coped with it without being healed in this area. God's timing and provision is perfect.'

Dave Tomlinson also had to go through a process in order to rediscover his own masculinity. His father was a dependent person unable to fulfil normal standard roles. He continues, 'I never doubted my father's masculinity or manhood. Masculinity therefore does not hinge on being a powerful, sustaining kind of person.

'It was the church and community which led me down the path of feeling that I had to be the provider and sustainer and the strong point of family unity. It has been a long and difficult road to get out of this and relearn. My wife's heart-cries, when I attempted to be this "all-sufficient" man showed I was dominating and squashing her personality. I was demanding her to be weak, when she could be strong.

'My "conversion" came at a "men only" conference, in which a man, who was by no means liberated himself made a statement out of the blue and said, effectively, that your wife is what you have made her! This penetrated me deeply and I cried as I realised that the way I had treated Pat and the expectations I had towards her, had in fact so changed her from the girl I had married. My mind was not yet enlightened and I was still seeing all this within a patriarchal framework, yet I made the quantum leap of wanting to find a way of relating which was more equal, giving her room and space for herself. So, for me, finding my masculinity has been entirely connected with the liberation of my wife. As I stop dominating, she has been able to discover who she is. This has at times been painful, but has been the road to self-discovery.'

Men can have grief over the remoteness of their fathers. They can still be trapped in a boyhood fear of abandonment, still believing that real manhood comes 'from' rather than 'through' the earthly father. It is God who leads through the darkness and shows the right road.

Men can also have grief and difficulty in relationships. As and when such suffering happens within the Christian experience, we become more Christ-like and are able to help others. Men also then become true heroes, with moral commitment, godliness and activism rather than seeking only fame or success.

Steve Chalke has been through a slow process of

appreciating that, rather than his security and masculinity being all tied up with how successful he was in what he did, it is bound up in relationships with his wife, children and the people close to him. He continues, 'Masculinity is not just found in achieving things, although to achieve in some areas is important. If I am unemployed, this does not mean I am less of a man. It is a question of defining what achievement means. We have taken on redundant men in Oasis and realised the blow of not having work leaves very deep feelings of uselessness and worthlessness.

'Ultimately, my security is in God. Most days I pray, "Lord, if I am a stumbling block in what I am doing, remove me from it!" However, the real test of this, would ultimately be in ceasing to do what I am doing. It is only then that I would finally know whether my security and masculinity are rooted in who I am rather than what I do.'

Phil Mohabir found his masculinity through his earthly father. His culture in South America promoted femininity in the young girl and masculinity in the young boy. He explains, 'I was taught how to be a responsible man from an early age, how to manage, how to be industrious and how to care for others. The girls were similarly taught, but protected from the more rigorous types of labour.

'I was also taught how to be an example to my younger brothers. My mother took time off to mould, teach and challenge me how to become a stable man and a responsible person in society. Today I find my security as to who I am and what I am, in Christ. My being and doing are rooted in Him.'

Dave Bilbrough is still in the process of finding out and does not feel he has arrived yet at the conclusion. He explains, 'My father first helped me to start to discover my masculinity and I am anxious to help my own sons develop their masculinity. My parents were very loving and helped me grow up to be open to Christ. They did not, however, help me to find Christ, so part of me was not "filled in" as a child.

'It was very important for me to write the song, "Abba Father", when I first came to grips with essential issues at the heart of my new faith. It is not coincidence that this is the first song I wrote. This was foundational in what I now do, and knowing the Father's love enables me to stand up and be a man. We can only find our true identity in God.'

Roger Forster believes that the father figure in the family is necessary to break the umbilical cord, for both son and daughter, from the mother whose bonds are so strong as she goes on caring. These bonds need to be lessened in order for the child to become an individual and so the mother's influence needs to be replaced more and more in later years by the father's.

Roger continues, 'The roles seem more locked into biological facts of the matter, rather than anything else. Much of the psychological writing on this matter seems a bit fanciful. I identified with my father in many areas including sport, which we did together. We had a friendship, and I regret that he died before I was married and was not there to help me understand my role as a husband. When I was young such things were not openly talked about. You deduced how things should be at home. My mother never went out to work while we were children. My father was very handy and every Sunday (after the roast dinner) he would clean the oven for the next week's cooking. I witnessed their partnership. He earned the money, she ran the house and cared for the children, but it never crossed my mind that he was intellectually superior to her. When a job had to be done, the one with experience and practice in that job did it. The roles are not definitive and you can get role reversal, if for example, the father is a cripple.

'My parents never squabbled in public or in front of us children and this gave me security. They were solidly there for us as we moved imperceptibly into adulthood, without thinking too much about it. Then we moved on into marriage and trying to understand our partners.

'You cannot have a proper love relationship

unless you share power equally. In a pair one cannot have three quarters of the power and the other a quarter. My parents modelled equality and I hope I have learned to be aware when I am not sharing power equally.

'God shares His power with us by mutual interaction on a fifty/fifty basis that makes a relationship. If God had made us somewhere between zero and fifty in the relationship with Him, He could have done a lot more and done it better and much more quickly. Yet He refused because a relationship cannot be built on a superiority/inferiority basis.

'The building of my relationship with my wife has given me a deeper understanding of how much she has given to establish my identity. I can understand myself better through being married to her, through being a father and through making the adjustments necessary to become a good man.

'Since my conversion, godly women have taught me and this has not been a problem. Archdeacon Guilleband's wife at Cambridge used to do Bible studies when I was converted. The idea of a woman not being able to teach the things of God never entered my head.

'Mrs McKenzie, whose husband disappeared one day on the mission field used to run the Bible College in Bexley Heath. After this traumatic event she continued her life following God and was a great teacher. These women had influence on me without my even recognising it. I grew and learned from God through these folk and found security and identity as a result.'

Charles Whitehead concludes this section by sharing something of his childhood. 'I went to a boarding school which was for boys only. This provided a strong masculine society, where it was assumed young masculine men would be produced. Men were authority figures and I would have found a certain security in that.

'Masculinity at school meant having a rational analytical way of thinking and acting. It meant taking responsibility for a household or the immediate social environment. My security came because I fitted into that pattern with my family background and school.

'Later in my teens I did begin to ask questions around this issue. I was questioning authority. I began to look at male authority and felt there was no reason for a woman not to exercise authority also. This brought me to thinking in terms of people, rather than men and women, and their characters, motivations and ideals in terms of what they did or owned. Looking behind what was visible, I would have found it difficult to articulate that I was beginning to look for the person.'

Men seem to move through confusion about their masculinity to a new place of relating to people on the basis of their humanity. They make mistakes and fail, but within the church, wounds can be healed. Some men have been influenced by feminism and the socialist movement, and feel they have discovered themselves, yet they exclude others of a different persuasion. Christian men have another option. Finding Christ is the beginning of dealing with male insecurity.

Jesus is our ultimate hero. He came as a man to show what God was like in His willingness to give up His own life and serve others. A woman could not have 'given up' power in that day and age in the same way. Jesus came as male, but not just masculine. He subverted wrong concepts of masculinity and showed men how to give up power in order to be whole. He was able at times to show feminine attributes. His identity and security were both derived from His relationship with the Father.

The Church needs to see that if Jesus is the normal man, then being a man is sufficient basis for the personality to display everything associated with being human. The characteristics of personality—both masculine and feminine are open to us all, as God has endowed each one. We can then begin to recognise one another as God's gifted children, each unique, all having one Father, without the stereotypes making us perform in certain ways.

CHAPTER THREE

Balanced Personality

IN OUR CULTURE there are those who think in terms of masculine and feminine traits being on two lists, each made up according to sexual characteristics. Others in our culture agree with Lenin who taught sexual sameness. Today the feminists' cry for equality has moved towards an assertion of sameness. However, often a woman is not as clearly understood as a man—she is more of a mystery. Men and women are not wholly instinct driven machines to be explained on the basis of biology alone. Social and cultural factors come into play, for example, menopausal women in Third World cultures do not appear to experience as much stress as their western counterparts. Their status increases with age.

We are not production machines. We make responsible decisions and actions. We cannot appeal to either biology or to learning to bypass our responsibility as men and women. Being created in God's image, we are morally accountable for how we live. A woman who blames her hormones for her rage or a man who blames his hormones for his lust have not understood that hormones do not rage or lust; they insinuate and permeate!

Most men take their masculinity for granted and as far as gender is concerned they often see themselves as persons rather than men. This affects their development and how they relate to people. Many have difficulty forming close male friendships, because of homosexual undertones. Others have lost contact with their 'feminine side' and try to add so called feminine qualities in reaction to feminism. How can a man effectively become whole with the right balance of masculine and feminine traits in his personality?

Gerald Coates begins by explaining that he feels the feminine needs to be released in men, because men do not make such good relationships as women do. This is partly because they often work nine to five, Monday to Friday, whereas many women have a little more flexibility. He continues, 'As traits of intuition such as the artistic or the sensitive re-emerge in men, men will become more whole as people.

'Defining masculine/feminine traits is difficult. A man wearing a dress here in England is not displaying a masculine trait and he probably needs a lot of help in his confused masculinity. In the Middle East, however, men wear robes and gowns. So we need to recognise cultural norms. In

Kampala, men walk down the main street hand in hand, yet women rarely link arms with women. Even in London, such behaviour amongst men out in the open would be unacceptable.

'The Bible asks us to abide by cultural norms so as not to bring disgrace to the gospel. Although culturally it is permissible to be warm and intimate and to touch people of the same sex in a semi-private setting, including greeting someone with a kiss, in Britain it is not acceptable to kiss in public in the way that it is in other parts of Europe. This is because you could be equating your life with homosexuality and if the freedom hinders the gospel, you have to ask, "Is it worth it?" '

Phil Mohabir believes that in every man there is a woman, as there is a woman in every man. He explains, 'We are none of us wholly masculine or feminine, however, I believe that men are more masculine than feminine and vice versa. My mother made me aware of this. I have a caring nurturing side to my character, yet no one will say that I am a feminine man. I like the gentle touch and yet I am capable of being a very rough person. I like things neat and tidy. I like flowers and I like to cook, although I have little time to develop my creativity in these areas at present.

'Being the eldest of my family with no older sisters, I cooked and washed, ironed and cleaned, as did all my six brothers. But I also learned to plough the fields. This certainly made life a lot richer for us. I learnt at an early age to appreciate the hard work and the burden that women bear in order to nurture society. In this I am not talking of just child bearing, but rather the many and varied tasks women perform in the home, whether married or single.'

Dave Bilbrough says that he feels that God is bigger than the masculine or the feminine and He created both aspects of character because He is both of them together. He continues, 'The male is not necessarily more of a reflection of God than the female. God speaks of being a father to the fatherless and also about being a mother in Isaiah. 66:13.

'I am aware of the other side of my personality. The question of my intuition is for me a key issue. As a musician, songwriter and worship leader, intuition is vital. In Scripture such people were to interpret the heart of God in a skilful way, therefore highly developed intuition is important. A songwriter thinks in terms of images and pictures rather than words and concepts. My intuition and feelings about things drew me to music initially, and as a musician I would like to develop this aspect of my personality even more.

'There is a debate in the evangelical church today concerning the role of worship leader. I feel that the worship leader tends to be leaning more towards the prophetic side of things. It requires intuition and certain feminine traits to put something into action musically.'

Steve Chalke is more aware of his intuition now and also trusts the gift in his wife. Ten years ago he would have discounted that aspect of her view of a situation. He shares, 'Recently, when looking for a new house, we found one which was fine. After the sale fell through my wife said that she was glad. For her, the house had had a bad feel about it.

'I now use my intuition more in particular situations with people, and in Oasis we now give the gift of intuition credence. Even dreams can be significant and I have shared my dreams at board meetings, when I felt they had real significance. God taught me the significance of dreams one year at Spring Harvest. I dreamed one of the leader's wives was ill during the weekend break. After the weekend, when I asked how things had gone, I was shocked to find it had been really hard for them, because she had been in bed the whole time. Now I take more notice of my dreams!'

John Noble feels that it is impossible to produce the definitive analysis of what is utterly masculine or completely feminine. He explains, 'There are certain times when my wife Christine, who is a great feeler, suddenly becomes frighteningly logical—for example when faced with demons or tax-inspectors! On the other hand I personally love my home and family and prefer to be there rather than travelling round the world in ministry. On yet another tack, my choice of clothes or fragrances may at times be quite feminine. I often find a sweater or a perfume in the ladies' department that I am quite happy to wear. On the whole, however, we fall into fairly classical roles and I am more than averagely masculine in my traits.

'Occasionally I do manifest a remarkable flash of intuition, but this serves to underline the incredible goodness of God at work in my life. For the most part I see myself as a kind of spiritual Frank Spencer! I go through life completely unaware of the chaos going on around me as a result of my lack of discernment and am very glad when Christine (my Betty) comes to my aid!'

We must, therefore, have an appreciation of how the feminine and the masculine complement each other. This link or affinity is essential for us to understand and work on the insecurities we have in our relationships. Men need to know they are men and appreciate their feminine side, without being threatened by it in given situations. It is the same for women, the other way round. If people decide that this complementing is just a pre-scientific superstition, it may be that they are trying to handle their insecurities, in saying that men and women are both the same.

Some people are both intuitive and feelers rather than thinkers. These attributes while both tending to be thought of as feminine are not the same. Intuition is the flash of insight, usually given in an instant, while feelings run deep and generally long term. Feelers cannot easily be proactive outside their feelings, whereas people with intuitive insights can have them and normally move on. How these things are manifested can vary culturally. Some are happy with limited overt expression. Some do not want to weep in public. Others become emotional over kindness, particularly when they themselves show kindness to others. Men must learn about their cultural conditioning and find the area where they are called to be responders, to become whole people.

Roger Forster comments that questioning whether God above all things is masculine may imply that receptivity and passivity are in some way inferior and lead to wrong conclusions. God accommodates His superiority to meet us where we are, because He loves us. This, to some degree, has to happen in all relationships to avoid the stronger exploiting the weak. That God has taken on Himself the name of Father may simply mean that the initiating activity of power and creativity is better expressed this way.

He continues, 'How we are biologically constructed has, it seems, made the woman genetically much more intuitive and the male much more reflective. (I do not like using the word rational, because it implies that woman are irrational, which is one hundred per cent wrong. When I was at university the first and most brilliant mathematician was a woman.) A woman is also more environmentally intuitive and is more open and alert to what is going on around her.

'Masculinity and feminity in each of us needs to come into being. My calling would be to develop the intuitive, because I find the rational reflective will develop anyway. Similarly women need to develop the reflective and logical side of their personalities, because the intuitive will develop itself.

'There are reasons why women develop intuition. One is that it is their first line of defence. The male's first line of defence biologically is in being physical, with his usually stronger body and larger shoulders. He is less vulnerable than a woman, who is often carrying a child, feeding a baby, bearing a child or menstruating. Her intuition is her guard in relationships, whereas a man can hit out at things in a macho manner. Jesus developed in a balanced way. He did what some would regard as feminine work. This is a challenge to us and we must make sure we are developing that other side of our being.'

Charles Whitehead feels that he has developed more intuitively probably over the last twenty years or so. However, rather than thinking of intuition as a more feminine trait, he now looks at it as part of some people's make-up more than others. He continues, 'I would still have to say that today most of the women I know are more intuitive than men. My wife picks up things more quickly than I do. I still see things very much at face value.

'It is not so necessary for men to be as intuitive as women who do more nurturing,and who develop that area of personality more deeply. My children have always made jokes like, "Mum's got eyes in the back of her head, but Dad if he is looking a certain way, only sees in that direction!"

'Having been brought up with a "stiff upper lip" mentality, I am aware that I am now more emotional than I used to be and things touch me more deeply than they used to do. God has opened up this repressed area for me, although it has taken time to move away from conventional attitudes.'

R. T. Kendall says, 'I think it is a false assumption to say that because someone has intuition they have a feminine trait. That may or may not be true. Personally, I think that I have some intuition, but I would not want to overstate nor over-estimate it.'

David Alton is aware of the other side of his personality. He says, 'The things that many men regard as being the essence of masculinity are some of the things that I dislike most, for example, aggression, a macho attitude and the need to dominate, whether it be found in men or women. Neither do I think that gentleness and sensitivity are the sole preserve of women. Men should not be frightened of such attributes or think them weak, trying always to be thick- skinned and hard-shelled. I feel a man who never allows these other traits to come through his personality is a lesser human being.'

Dave Tomlinson concludes by saying that he is aware that slowly but surely he is developing in new ways. He explains, 'A critical time for us was when both Pat and I were going to the office to work and the children were nearly grown. Coming home I would still expect her to fulfil all the housewifely roles, while I sat down. Realising that I had to do something about this, I began to take my fair share of the responsibilities. The thing I wanted to have a go at was cooking, which I had never attempted before. I am now the main cook in the house, and have developed this over five or so years. Aspects of my personality have been developed in this too. I cannot easily cook if, for example, I am feeling aggressive. I have to slow down and become absorbed in a gentle task.

'This has been a very liberating avenue of creativity. Intuitively, my development has been slower. I tend to take people at face value, whereas Pat is much better than me in this area of intuition I still very much need to listen to her as part of the team.'

Many men today are now realising that family is more important than work. Work, for them, is no longer the area in which to prove they are men. Jesus is our model, because He displays the range of human characteristics and gifts available to men and women starting with relationships. In Jesus we find God's restored humanity, for us all.

Christian men who are becoming aware of their masculinity are on a pilgrimage. Their healed masculinity is part of their restored humanity. They have also to discover other aspects of their personality. Christ conveys in one personality a whole range of strengths. It is wrong to equate God with maleness. He is asexual, both male and female. Sexuality is not an issue in the Godhead. Mankind is, therefore, not to be split rigidly into two groups according to our limited understanding of sexual characteristics. A man is sexually male but in his personality he will have both masculine and feminine characteristics.

Jesus was incarnate as a man in a way which was both right for His time and right for His primary purpose of showing forth the new concept of the Father's love. Therefore, we worship God as

Father, and rightly so. But God also dwells in us men and women, by His Spirit, who is altogether masculine and feminine. We are all, therefore, capable of both masculine and feminine actions. When God took Eve out of Adam, He left it to them to work out the facets of their particular relationship as they moved on to have dominion together.

For a woman to be truly appreciated as a woman by a man, without the feminist or sexual connotations, man must begin discovering who he is. In partnerships and marriages we start a process of learning. A part of this is a man learning about the feminine side of his character. If a man does not know himself, he does not listen or generally hear a woman. He tends to think women are illogical and wrong. He has not understood anything other than his incomplete perspective that his world view, so he thinks, is the only right and logical one!

MEN IN RELATIONSHIP TO THEIR FAILURES

CHAPTER FOUR

Chauvinism

MUCH IS MADE OF male chauvinism today. Some people assume all men have chauvinism to overcome. They see a genetic flaw in males, which makes it all too easy for a man to assume that he has the right to dominate a woman. They also see, in women, the temptation to avoid risks that might upset relationships, as a genetic flaw which gives space to man to dominate even more. Some Christian men see their roles as having the divine sanction of dominance, yet New Testament submission is based on respect, not obedience. Their Christian women say that it is more peaceful to submit consistently to a husband, and they become content with peace without justice. Slaves too have been content, but their situation is not just.

The issue of male chauvinism and power needs therefore to be addressed to find if there are ways through the maze to reasonable conclusions. Is there a balance that can be found to bring men and women happily together, when the irony of the situation today is that men are re-evaluating the stress of work, while women still have to prove themselves?

R. T. Kendall starts by saying, 'I feel that the issue is not so much overcoming chauvinism as developing respect for women. You do not surrender your own sense of security by affirming a woman!'

Roger Forster explains that Adam blamed Eve in Genesis, before God, but Eve did not blame Adam but rather the serpent, which was intuitively a far better assessment of the situation.

He continues, 'I have heard a male expositor say that when Joseph fled from Potiphar's wife it was a wonderful thing, afterwards implying that Potiphar's wife and all women in the world were there just to seduce men if possible! Women, therefore, become the great threat to males and if a man falls it is the woman's fault!

'Another example that comes to mind is that of Adoniram Judson who was imprisoned. His first wife did such a tremendous job to get him released while maintaining the work. Yet people eulogise him and never say a word about his wife who did the major part of the work. So it seems that if there is success in a man's life, he gets the accolade, and if there is failure the woman takes the blame. We blame each other when we do not get things right.

'Sometimes in church life, we males can be

destructive in giving in to our dispositions, thinking we have got power, therefore, *ipso facto*, we can often use it without thinking too closely about the people we may be harming in our decision making. I cannot at present show that chauvinism is a part of my character, however, I am quite sure it is true. Often my wife has helped me to think about personal feelings and responses that are likely in a person who has not got power and this has been very helpful to me. She has probably had a considerable part to play in identifying anything of chauvinism which might arise in me. We do not understand the opposite sex until we are close enough to work out a relationship with them. In understanding the opposite sex, we are helped to understand ourselves.

'Women who have positions of power also have a similar problem although they do think more about the person involved. So finally, I am not clear whether the issue is that power corrupts. The issue is using power, but not putting oneself into the position of the powerless. Perhaps it is also the case that women who have so often been the underdog can more quickly spot the issue.'

Gerald Coates' greatest personal help in this issue is the role model of Jesus Christ. He continues, 'In the story of the Samaritan woman, Jesus seems to bite the bullet of racism, sexism and nationalism all in one go. In the story of the woman taken in adultery, Jesus used incredible wisdom and realised this was pure sexism, because adultery requires a man and a woman! He offered the woman hope and forgiveness for her wrong and asked her not to do it again. This story shows me that you deal with people as people and not women differently from men. All human beings deserve dignity and respect.

There are still grave inconsistencies today. The use of exclusive language by preachers such as, "Where are the men who want to serve God?" or "God has got His hand on the men of this nation," gives an impression that fifty per cent of the nation does not exist and that God cannot use women in any way at all. Jackie Pullinger was speaking in Durban, South Africa some weeks after I spoke there at City Hall and I reminded the people with some passion that famous as she was for her apostolic work which they would flock to hear about, she could not be a house group leader if she lived in South Africa.'

Phil Mohabir is clear that male chauvinism is rooted in pride, with a lack of appreciation of the worth and value of womankind. He believes it is a deep insult to God's beautiful creation, and he does not just mean 'skin-deep' beauty. He explains, 'If I believe a woman is created in the image and likeness of God and equally redeemed by the blood of Jesus and yet I treat her as something of less value, this insults Jesus sacrifice on the cross.

'I would not claim that I have totally overcome in this issue and would not hold myself up as a model. We all have our failures, but I do overcome by seeking to have a true appreciation of the value and worth of a woman. She is one of God's children and someone who is equal. We need one another in partnership, valuing each other's opinions and perspectives on life. God made it that way, He said, "It is not good for man to be alone." Neither a man nor a woman is the better and so a woman cannot be my slave rather only my complement.

'Men as well as women have to work at human relationships. They have been conditioned against emotions and have despised them, yet they still have feelings. They need to see that women are not intellectually inferior to them; they just have not been given the opportunity in times past to develop in the way that men have. We all need restoration.'

In political life, **David Alton** sometimes sees people using their own power in destructive ways. He opposes this, whether it comes from men or women. He also feels that people in Parliament should be chosen on the basis of merit. He explains, 'When I was chairman of the Liberal Party's Candidates Committee, it was clear to me that many women were not even coming through the starting gate, which was the selection short-list. I introduced the idea that there should always be a woman on that short list, so that suitable women would have to be head-hunted. This resulted in a higher number of women being put up as candidates.

'Liverpool is an interesting city from which to draw experience. I have represented people there for over twenty years and often feel that many of the problems there are caused by aggressive males. Some of the militant leaders of the recent past acted in a macho way, because they believed they could railroad through their own brand of ideology. In taking on the government they behaved like supporters in a football match deter-mined to knock their opponents out of the cup, instead of looking to find ways of trying to resolve the problems in co-operation and partnership. A false sense of the macho-man led to using the city as a battering ram against the central govern-ment.

'The men in Liverpool remind me of the men in the New Testament. Peter, who was one of the great men, was like most of us, a fairly flawed indi-vidual. He could be a loud mouth promising much, but when the crunch came, he was nowhere to be seen. He was quite a contrast with many of the New Testament women.'

Some men come to terms with this whole issue when young teenagers. They see destructive chauvinistic male authority in the families around them. A man might be treated as god in his own house and this can then be seen as wrong. If another man has been lucky enough to have both parents working well together in a partnership this too is a strong model against chauvinism.

So some make the move from being a controlling leader to being a more consensus-seeking style of leader. Sometimes admitting failure is part of the process. This can result in developing from an all sufficient person to one who trust others and works co-operatively in equal partnerships.

Dave Bilbrough has walked this path. 'Culturally, I have probably some male chauvinistic tendencies within me. Coming from the house church movement, fifteen years ago the whole emphasis was on men taking their place and fulfilling their role. I would like to think that I was not chauvinistic now having come to a balanced view of neither making men pre-eminent nor just promoting women. The issue is the recognition of one another's gifts.

'Being married I appreciate my wife's gifts, particularly where she is more gifted than I. When you are close to a person, you see their gifts not as a threat but rather as enhancing your life.

Although I am quite intuitive, Pat's intuition is more finely tuned than mine, and can be used in certain areas to great benefit. This has probably further helped me to overcome chauvinism.'

For **John Noble** overcoming chauvinism has been a slow steady work of grace, with three facets. 'Firstly, the scriptures kept confronting my preconceptions and Christian conditioning. Secondly, contemporary women and women in history were visible to me with their God-given gifts. Thirdly, my wife refused to stop asking awkward questions. All these conspired to move me from believing the Church's greatest problems stemmed from strong women to seeing that so many of today's failures can be traced back to weak men, who seek to dominate women so that their own lack of response to God remains hidden. Once I saw this I realised that far from being a threat, women were my greatest allies. Their skills, loyalty, and no-fuss approach to so many simple or even menial tasks put most men to shame.'

Steve Chalke is also aware of the destructive use of power. He explains, 'God has given me a personality whereby I seem to be able to lead others, which has both strengths and weaknesses. For instance, in my marriage I can out-talk and out-logic my wife on anything. This is what a preacher is! You can invent logical argument, even if you have not got one! Out-talking is my weakness and I know it.

'Within Oasis I tend not to think of people as men and women. We have appointed people to positions because they are suited for that particular role, and whether they are male or female has not been part of the issue. I hope we are providing a good model for others on this issue now.'

Tony Higton feels that male chauvinism is rooted in a sense of threat, whereby men build protective walls around themselves to keep people in general and women in particular, at a slight distance, in order that their own weaknesses cannot be seen. He continues, 'I am not convinced that I have entirely overcome male chauvinism although I would not consciously entertain it, because it is quite wrong, hurtful and unchristian. However, these things run deep. The Bible has a very positive attitude towards women and it is not, therefore, open to me to be a male chauvinist.

'As an insecure person in early adult life, I have had to work through the "threat" of having a wife who is very competent and perceptive. But had this problem not been there for me, we would still have had to work things through. We have now reached a mature and relaxed relationship.

'I have seen the damage that male chauvinism has done to women and how they are "put down" both deliberately and thoughtlessly. I have at times been annoyed by the unnecessary and insensitive exclusion of women from discussions. I also react against women wanting to perpetuate an inferior servile status. I personally believe in an overall male authority in the Church, but an authority that will liberate those who are under it. This is the test as to whether leadership is authoritarian or not.'

Joel Edwards feels that he needs someone else to tell him how they think he has overcome the potentially destructive use of male power. He concludes, 'I am aware of the need to face it and deal with it in the same way that we need to overcome racism. I do not think that I will ever be able to safely claim that I have overcome in this area, but rather I feel I am in a process of entertaining a consciousness of it and being vigilant about my own attitude to women.

'There are times, during my pastoral work for example, when I believe I am working with sensitivity towards women and a woman in the group castigates men's attitude towards women. I then feel that she cannot be talking about me, because I am doing my best for the cause of women! The result is that I am caught, taken aback and have to look again at my attitudes. This is an ongoing process, yet looking at my ministry and comparing it with my contemporaries in the same denominational stable, I feel that we do not do too badly in this area. We have a strong female attendance, with many women who keep me on my toes so to speak!'

Some Christians feel that Adam was dominant because he named Eve. However, his recognition of a wonderful addition to his life, because he was 'not good alone', drew this naming of her as 'bone of my bone, flesh of my flesh'. He recognised their sameness and understood their difference. They were secure equals. God then commanded them to rule the earth together.

After the Fall, female subordination was the result of sin. However, to sanctify male dominance in the Church would be to turn the outcome of the Fall into the norm, without working through the consequences of redemption. We in the Church cannot give in to such power which comes from a source of evil. It must be dealt with and we then become sanctified in this area.

Our key, therefore, is to look to Christ. Christian men must behave in a christian way. In redemption God reverses the effect of the Fall and buys back what is already His. We must partake of this redemption and then work through the consequences, sometimes with pain. Then people in the world will begin to see something of our potential for wholeness in the kingdom of God.

CHAPTER FIVE

Deception

WHAT IS DECEPTION? Is it what you do to someone else or is it the capacity to be deceived? There are many kinds of deception and mostly they fall into three main catagories: money, sex and power. Many people are deceivers in these areas and many more people are thus deceived, with the newspapers full of their stories.

Christians too can be conned. False claims are made in order to get people to give money. Close friends have suddenly found that one of them has left a wife or husband to go off with another. Power is wielded in a company structure as a basis of who you know in a club, which is really nothing to do with the company. The examples are many.

Many are deceived because they believe what their leader tells them. If the issues are not thought through it is easy to be gullible. This is particularly true if the leaders are powerful personalities and the people do not really think for themselves.

John Noble helps us to understand that even superficial research of cults and false religions will reveal that the vast majority have been started and perpetuated by men. He says, 'Pick up your concordance and check out the theme of deception in both Old and New Testaments and you will discover that by far the highest proportion of references to deception apply to men. If women are more vulnerable to deception as some claim, this weakness must have been put there by God at creation, which to me is a horrendous thought. How could God create a perfect being with such a weakness? Had He done that, at least Eve's part in the Fall would be God's responsibility. No, men and women were simply given the freedom to choose by God, and they both chose to do wrong.

'One of the greatest deceptions of all time is the incredible way in which Satan has beguiled us men into believing that women are the prime danger in this connection and that men should under all circumstances control things. The evidence of the enormity of this deception can be seen on every hand. Look at the tragic mess men have made trying to govern without the help and input of women, not only in the world, but in the Church as well. For some years I too was sucked into believing this lie, which fostered feelings of superiority and pride in me, which I never admitted. Like most men I could always find a good reason why men's ideas and plans failed, but if a woman made a mess of things it had to be because she was a woman, and after all what else could you expect!'

David Alton knows that we are all open to deception because the great deceiver is at work in society. He comments, 'C. S. Lewis's *Screwtape Letters* amply shows how the Devil is constantly at work trying to deceive people. Women are no more prone to this than men. Personally, during my struggle over the abortion legislation, one thing that struck me again and again was that when the opinion polls were conducted and the meetings held, there were always far more women present in support than men.

'One day, in a Manchester bookshop, a young man approached me most angrily. He attacked me because my attempts at changing the law would have stopped the woman he had made pregnant from having an abortion. When I asked him why the abortion was necessary, he replied that a baby would have ruined his career! It was clear that he had forced her into having an abortion and maybe his anger was caused by some sense of guilt at having done so. He was pushing all the responsibility onto her, and wrongly believed that it was purely a matter for her which had nothing to do with him.

Men can deceive themselves and push things onto women which are equally their responsibility.'

Tony Higton also finds it difficult to believe that women are more deceived than men and does not think that Paul was saying this in 1 Timothy 2:14. 'He was stating the fact that Eve was the one who happened to be deceived by Satan, and she then led Adam (by persuasion) into sin. It could have happened the other way round. Paul's interest was in Eve wrongly taking a lead, hence its relevance to the context.

'I have seen a good deal of male deception. Many heretics and false prophets are male. I have also known married men including clergy who have been quite convinced that God has brought another woman into their lives and that their wife was never the right person for them! This moral deception I see as emotional based on sexual feelings, and a self-deception which stems from wanting to believe something other than the truth.'

Charles Whitehead is aware that he would tend to be more easily deceived by a woman than by a man. He also believes that probably a woman is more easily deceived by a man rather than by another woman. 'My own experience of male deception has been within the business world, where people lead each other "up the garden path" out of motives of self-interest or personal profit. It eventually becomes a question of when do you appreciate that this has been happening to you? I have made mistakes in believing people when they have not been strictly honest. One instance that particularly comes to mind was when I was dealing with a more feminine type of man.

'I have also been led "up the garden path" by women who have had an agenda that I have not recognised at the time. People are deceived by those who are plausible, or liars *per se*. However, I cannot say that I believe that women are more easily deceived than men. It may be that I personally understand the signals better from the more masculine type of man and am able to see their lack of subtlety .'

Joel Edwards also does not believe women to be more easily deceived than men. In his experience it is usually the other way around. 'In the areas of moral deception, character assessment and truth versus falsehood, women tend to be more practical, and therefore look out for things which men either take for granted or miss altogether. As a result they are much less susceptible to deception.

'In the classical reference to Adam and Eve we can misunderstand the true situation. Eve was not as immediately accountable, therefore she was more susceptible to be conned than Adam, who received a direct command. Others would say that in a strange way Adam was far more fallible than Eve.

'I feel the greatest deception for men is self-deception. Men often confuse superiority with accountability and live insecure lives. This can happen in and out of the Church and such men live burdened by the lie of a superiority complex. They then become threatened if challenged, even in such things as a game of tennis or chess when a woman wins. If you are convinced that a black person is inherently inferior for example, it is just not right for them to do anything better than you! This produces patronising attitudes such as "He speaks very well for a black person!" Patronising attitudes are similarly found in relation to the gender issue.'

Some men are conscious that their wives are highly intuitive, and yet not quite as hard-bitten as they are because of their work in a world where someone is always trying to sell you something, and where you have to learn the difference between the sales talk and the truth, and continually make quick decisions.

Some men feel women tend to express emotion more easily, and that as they are intuitive in picking up things they can draw wrong conclusions. Yet there are many sharp logical women, just as there are many irrational, confused and subjective men! Even so, some men prefer to have logical men around so that, they hope, deception is less possible. However, the power to deceive is sometimes wielded by men who think in terms of concepts and systems, which women sometimes find threatening. Had intuitive women been alongside such male thinkers, deceptive power might have been unmasked and therefore far less influential.

Another form of deception lies within the issue of homosexuality. The child within has a legitimate need to affirm relationships with the parent and other people, of the same sex in order to gain a sense of self-worth. A hatred of a distant or nonexistent father means there is no celebration of maleness for men. Trying to find their male sexual identity, they often split off from their true masculinity. A God-given release from the hurt can lead to a liberation of gender and a way out of this deception.

Gerald Coates feels it is sheer lunacy to say that women are more easily deceived than men. The majority of heresies that have come into this country have been perpetuated by men. 'One of the simple reasons is that men have almost all the power in leadership. It is amazing to me that women, who have had no training and no opportunity to be in any leadership forum, have not created more heresy by way of reaction!

'If we really believe that women are more easily deceived, then why is it that women are asked to look after our children in Sunday schools, particularly between the ages of five through to fifteen? They are often not monitored by men. Deception comes firstly through a lack of understanding of Scripture, secondly through a lack of fellowship with other people who would modify perspectives, and thirdly through sin. If I have an affair, fiddle my tax or gossip about someone, I have to compartmentalise my life and cover my tracks with lies and deception. Experience tells me men are more susceptible to this than women.'

Phil Mohabir thinks that those who feel women are more easily deceived than men are partly conditioned by society's thinking. 'Eve was the first one to listen to the serpent, yet if Adam was stronger and superior, we have to ask how he succumbed? There was no excuse for Adam falling into disobedience. Blaming Eve did not let him off the hook. This is apparent in the way God judged the situation in the Garden of Eden.

'For every woman who has been deceived you will also find a man. I know many men who have been deceived, often by their own sense of importance in their Christian work. One man I know was tremendously anointed and used by God in miracles, signs and wonders and yet he went into error and heresy. As a result thousands of people were misled.

'I know of others who had the call of God on their lives and started out well, but this went to their heads and they became lifted up in pride, assuming that which God never gave them. Their effectiveness withered and they became more of a stumbling block than a blessing.

'I also know of cases where Christian men have

used their influence to seduce women. Moral deception often starts when pride enters the heart of a man who thinks he is the chosen servant of God, immune from error. The most common areas of deception for men are along the lines of truth, sexual morality, and money.'

Dave Tomlinson has observed that men are more easily deceived than women. He feels that we have had stereotyped roles that have been expected of both sexes, women towards the more intuitive and men towards the more rational basis. He explains, 'To have a partnership between rational and intuitive is difficult. I have worked with Phil Mohabir, a very intuitive person, who sometimes feels things quite strongly. In the course of our work, he has sometimes been unable to rationalise his strong feelings; decisions have been made on the basis of my reason, rather than on that of his intuition and we have undoubtedly lived at times to regret this. So this issue is not always just a male–female one.

'If we men had been able to listen more to our wives, we could have saved ourselves and everybody else a lot of problems. I still maintain that it is preposterous to say that women are more open to deception than men. As women are taking more and more opportunities and being trained, for example, to teach theology rationally, those who do it do so at least on equal terms with men.'

R. T. Kendall feels that at the natural level, men are the more deceived. He says, 'At the spiritual level, one can be given discernment and whoever has that gift can be decidedly on top form, whether male or female. The greatest hurts in my life have been in relation to male authority figures whom I have known and trusted, but who betrayed me.'

Roger Forster concludes with strong words. 'It is absolutely ludicrous to say that because Eve was deceived, all women from then on would also be deceived and, therefore, they must not be teachers. A question I often ask is whether it is better to have a woman to lead, who you think might be easily deceived, or a man to lead who believes that he is not deceived and deliberately does what is wrong. Which situation is the most devastating? Eve was not there when the first command was given, so she had it secondhand from Adam and he should have taken more responsibility, but he did not do so.

'It is a very serious statement to say that women are more easily deceived than men, especially if you base it on the assumption that the intuitive nature often predominates in women and the reflective logical side predominates in men. The intuitive, sincere person, seeming to hear from God, is far better than the deducer, who after a series of propositions and statements, might well be miles off course, through wrong logical reflections. I would much rather hear from God who tells us to do something which we do not understand logically at the time, and continue to do it, until in retrospect we understand.

'The Greek way of thinking (which is the more masculine activity) has predominated in Western society. The intuitive way of thinking is found far more in the Bible and amongst the Hebrews. This means that you have to be engaged with the truth rather than looking at the truth in a detached way. It is by doing that we really know something and as Jesus said, "If any man is willing to do my Father's will, he shall know...". The doing of what God is commanding is the means by which I come to know what it means.

'The whole issue of Western protestant theological thought, including current charismatic issues, is dominated by the Greek form of thinking. This has been cultured and purpetuated through Western society, from the earliest days of Christianity in Europe. In the past, however, it was not so prominent, which leads me to believe it may just be that males had the grip of scholarship in their hands and promoted the Greek and Latin philosophers and classics in the Renaissance, and so they dominated theology with it, including the male female issues.

'Marx's step forward in philosophy, popularly called "the praxis", that we only learn and know by doing, needs to be heard. Becoming involved may mean taking your first step intuitively because you hear from God intuitively. Later logical assessment can take place. This issue of how we know anything is very important. If Eve being created second prohibits her teaching, then logically every older person should teach every younger. It is preposterous to say that this issue is a male–female one. The text doesn't say that it is rather talking about first and second.

'Most heresies have been brought into being through males. Most of these are to do with male logic in the theological field. Men think they can be objective, stand back and work out a truth without engaging in it. As a result, the mass of deception has come from them, and not so much from women!

'Looking at the other side, the intuitive gut feelings of the Quakers or Methodists against slavery, even though there are verses teaching about slaves in the Bible, began to deal with this issue. Today we have a logical hermeneutic which demonstrates that the Bible does not teach slavery, in fact it emancipates slaves. As Jesus told us, "He came to set the captives free." It is, therefore, essential to have the intuitive side of the issue there first, before the logical argument is worked out.

'The same is true on the gender issue. Like most males, when I was converted and began to read scripture I was confronted with the difficult passage in 1 Timothy 2 . I had to ask myself if this was what was really being said in the light of the rest of the Bible. My spiritual intuition on it (as with the slavery issue) drew me to a different conclusion from some other people.'

This whole area of deception inside the male–female issue is fraught. We have a natural drive towards intimate communion, yet our acceptance of one another is affected by our insecurities and fears of one another's gifts. A strong woman can be labelled a 'controlling Jezebel' by weak, insecure men, when there is no sexual immorality whatsoever. Revelation 2:21 states that this is part of that syndrome. It may be that the immorality is in the heart of those trying themselves to control the woman, and thus they are self-deceived.

The mind transforms unacceptable impulses into their opposite and so we get the pastor against pornography. We deny unacceptable impulses in ourselves by attributing them to others and so the work of deception begins. If I expect blessing, then blessing is on the forefront of my mind. If, however, I expect harm then I refuse to talk about the harmful thing, displacing any suggestion of its activity in me and becoming self-righteous about exposing others, who have not boxed up this negative idol in their lives, whether it be money, sex or power.

We are all equally capable of falling into these

deceptions. To say however, that a woman is more likely to do so, for me is to underline the fact that those who say this are generally the remaining insecure men who control the *status quo*. They fear above all else that they have been wrong and will be found out!

In His judgement in the garden of Eden, God never implied that Eve was in league with Satan. In fact, He said that he would put distance between Eve and Satan, stating, 'I will put enmity between you and woman', in Genesis 3:15. Adam never saw Satan in the frame and blamed God for giving him Eve!

Yet the bad character of Adam in this matter has not meant all men being disqualified from leadership! The Bible makes much of Adam's guilt, but little of Eve's transgression in both Old and New Testaments. God, in fact, continues in the Garden of Eden to say that through Eve's seed deliverance shall come. Adam may well have understood something of this, because he named his wife 'Eve' after God's statement concerning her seed. She was certainly to be a fit helper for him as some translations of Genesis 2:18 imply 'a power equal to him.' The very fact that many women are intuitive, particularly in spiritual things, is of itself a very powerful aid against deception and the works of the enemy.

CHAPTER SIX

Passivity

HISTORICALLY, PASSIVITY has been seen as a more feminine trait and recognised as an extension of a woman's response to the initiating male. Today many men are seen as passive and therefore feminised. There are two factors which are important in the debate about the so-called feminisation of the Church. One is that if the Church is filled up with the outcasts of society or the put-down class of females, this is our strength. The good news is always for the poor and the disadvantaged. The other factor is that, in spite of all the psychological aspects of the problem, men do relax into a passivity, probably to have peace and quiet.

A woman, however, from bearing children, has a very aggressive aspect to her character and will fight for them as and when necessary. This is in spite of initial passivity in being the receptive rather than pro-active vehicle in sexual activity. We also see the desire in the woman to bring into order things which are out of order. She intuitively moves to solve her problems. If a woman moves into passivity here, it is usually in order to save relationships, and she can as a result become manipulative.

If we understood each other a little better, and the fighting woman was a little slower and the passive male was given a little more space to do his logical reflection, then maybe we would get on better together and resolve more problems. The alternative is increasing polarisation, each driving the other further away. The result can be a man allowing a woman to dominate with him becoming an absent or silent partner.

Tony Higton made a decision in his mid-teens no longer to be passive and he is now a workaholic! 'If I believe something is right, I want to go for it rather than sit around wishing and hoping. Scripture says that we should not let sin have dominion over us and obviously we do not overcome passivity by will-power alone. Yet the importance of the will is underestimated today. In the New Testament, men are told to love their wives, as an act of the will, because feelings wax and wane. Today love is often thought of as a sloppy sentiment, but in scripture it is primarily an act of will. Many marriages could be saved if couples were properly counselled about this, yet we do not teach this, to our cost.

'Some people have gone into legalism or a do- it-yourself Christianity, which we also need to avoid.

110

We often find a 'consumer gospel' (come to Jesus and receive all the blessings), but this is not the heart of the gospel. Rather, we are called to love God with our whole being and to receive justification by grace through faith, which includes repentance. We must not breed a generation of Christians who are into Christianity for what they can get out of it, whether it be salvation, healing or even prosperity! Neither should we encourage the idea that Christians cannot obey God without constant counselling, inner healing and deliverance, whatever place those ministries may have within the Church.'

Dave Tomlinson is not aware that he has been subject to passivity. He says 'I am not aware of passivity, yet I feel that I may well be learning something more of it in a right sense, in that I do not have to be all-sufficient or have all the answers. This may well be a good swing of the pendulum.'

Phil Mohabir knows a lot of men who need to take more initiative with positive action. Too many are passive, laid back, looking for an easy lifestyle and lacking a sense of responsibility. He continues, 'I am overactive but passivity is one of the major contributors to the degeneration of society. We do not have masculine (as opposed to muscular) men taking initiative with responsibility. As a result today, fatherhood is such a poor thing, often the missing ingredient in society.

'To overcome in this, men must recognise that God has a purpose for them, which is conceived in love. They need to catch a vision of their own potential in God with the sky being the limit. God wants a life full of meaning. Knowing this will go a long way to move people out of their passivity.

'We can be affected by the more aggressive feminists and think, "Why should I bother?" or "Let them get on with it!" Men as well as women need appreciation to bring out the best in them and they often feel unappreciated and undervalued. Human beings work better with encouragement. We all need to be affirmed.'

Dave Bilbrough feels that there are two types of passivity. He explains, 'One comes from God, when at times He tells us to wait on Him. The other kind is not taking our rightful place, which God has given. Every time I write a song, after the intial God-given inspiration comes a time of passivity, when it seems that the task is overwhelming. The more songs I write, the harder it becomes. The task can seem more and more daunting.

'Passivity is best overcome by calling on inner resources, by saying that God is at work in your life, that He has chosen you for a purpose and given you the gifts that are necessary. Constantly reminding ourselves of our own self-worth enables us to make a contribution. In the past I have made the mistake of standing back, whereas others got on with things. I tend to be the kind of person who won't do anything unless God speaks. The result is that strength becomes weakness. The antidote to this is to know that God is at work in your life.'

John Noble is still aware of passivity at times in his life, particularly in dealing with problems or taking difficult decisions. He says, 'I easily slip into the "If I leave it, it might go away" mode. Doing this produces fear and frustration in my wife, family or the Church as the case may be. I am then threatened by those who feel the need to take action and step into the vacuum which I have created.

'I now try to clearly identify situations which need to be addressed urgently. I pray and consult, seeking my wife's advice and input or that of trusted people in the team or church. If a decision is mine to make I will then make it, being willing to take responsibility for the outcome personally.

'Most people are willing to follow when prayer and consultation have taken place, but asking them to agree with you can be too much. Weaker men in leadership demand this, but it is more than folks can or should give. Such emotional pressure at best produces spiritual zombies and at worst it breeds rebellion.'

Charles Whitehead says that for him passivity is not an issue, although he sees this as a problem for many people. 'There are a lot of people who do not want to make decisions or take responsibility for anything. They respond passively. Dominant leadership often produces this type of person, who is used to being told what to do all the time.

'There have been times when I have entered into a new circle of work and been amongst people who seemed to know a lot more than I did. This can be the time to keep your head down and learn. This is not passivity but rather a deliberate silence until one has learned and gained in experience and knowledge.'

He explains further, 'It is also true to say that there is a right passivity, as that which Paul required of new young illiterate women in the church in the 1 Timothy 2 passage. The Bible also says that there is a time to speak and a time to be silent and whilst we are learning, silence cannot be called passivity.

'Some men are passive because they feel they cannot win. They feel too much is expected of them and as a result bypass responsibility and live self-interested lives. Others master their passivity in various ways hoping the issue will go away, or they create difficulties when they do not have agreement on an issue.'

Joel Edwards says he has never been passive nor

has he been pushy. 'I am somewhere between the two. I respond to opportunities as they present themselves. I would not describe myself as ambitious, but neither am I afraid to step forward to make a contribution, especially if it is something which I feel strongly about. My motivation often comes from asking myself questions such as "What am I doing here?" or "Why am I doing this?" or "What makes you qualified to be doing what you are doing?" '

Passivity has not been a problem for **David Alton**. He feels that he is sometimes hyperactive and needs to slow down. 'I understand passivity from my surgery in Liverpool. It is mostly the women who come to sort out the family problems. The men are often disinterested, not regarding it as their job. Society has allowed these compartments to be created, with the feminist movement on occasions contributing to this problem. For example, when it is said that abortion is soley a woman's issue, it lets men off the hook and they do not take responsibility for something which is half their making. The women at the cross remind me of the matriarchs of Liverpool. They alone, with the exception of John, accompanied Jesus to the cross, stayed with him to the end and sorted out the details of his burial.'

Steve Chalke comments, 'Passivity is not one of

my character traits. I tend to get into something and then have to see it through! I think I have inherited this from my father. Once I've got the bit between my teeth, I tend to take things to the "nth" degree if necessary. Like all character traits this has its good side as well as its downside.'

Gerald Coates feels that passivity has not been his personal problem. He concludes, 'Most people are passive but only in certain areas, because we all have to specialise. When the Spirit of God comes into your life, He cleanses what is impure, fills what is empty and begins to illuminate and create in the areas where there has been passivity. Often within human relationships passivity can be found through fear of rejection or fear of being wrong. When the love of God comes in, you can afford to take steps out into the world even if you are unsure or laughed at, because you know that you are loved.

'Many people are passive because they feel that they have not been empowered to do anything. As my friend Tom Marshall said, "If you are a leader, do you really have power when you are leading one hundred powerless people!?" We need to empower people through affirmation, confirmation and even legislation.'

So we conclude, seeing that there is much to be done. Having interviewed leaders who are initiators, we naturally find that they personally do not have a great problem with passivity! Yet an insecure man who may be afraid of losing his wife may not show anger and may become passive, being easily manipulated with a fear of responsibility. Some say that men only see anger as destructive and painful and as a result become overly feminised. Yet Christian men can have the capacity to love their wives and be angry without sinning.

Women need decisive rather than passive men, for their own well-being even if they are decisively wrong at times. This means involvement, and sometimes angry words. Some men remain passive, having learned this when young in order to avoid their own hostility towards their mothers. They have often withdrawn from their fathers too and need healing for these wounds which developed whilst they were growing up.

A genuine desire to please both God and one's wife can engender strength within a man. He can begin to overcome his fears and move out into full masculine maturity. This blessing produces fulfilment for the individual, meaningful relationships with a future and purpose in God that counts for eternity.

MEN IN RELATIONSHIP TO THE CHURCH

CHAPTER SEVEN

Secure Men

OUR CULTURE GIVES men little validation of their manhood, compared to many other cultures. The masculine warrior is no longer the hero that he was except in the Rambo-like image, which is an illusion. A youth who does not confirm his manhood within the larger community of men through his father may well seek it elsewhere with for example, woman after woman. This too is an illusion.

Men are fighters by nature and have innate tendencies to violence. This is not, however, tamed by losing masculinity. Men in conflict often show that their anger is still there and they can push themselves to the point of physical exhaustion in an effort to measure up to the so-called standard! Yet often the more success a man achieves, the more he tends to lose male fellowship and the validation that goes with it.

Men can also be confused over their life goals, often as a result of poor bonding with their fathers. Wrong bonding with a mother can trap a young adult male into fear concerning a possible move in a certain direction. A distant or non-existent father is no help in this matter. Does the church today have answers for our generation of men who, when coming to know God as Father need to make major adjustments, in order to become what they were intended to be?

Joel Edwards feels that he facilitates insecure men rather than secure men! He explains, 'Many men are dysfunctional underachievers. Pastorally, I find many women having to sit back and look at men who are not always functioning adequately. However, when one finds a secure man with some gifting, I want to facilitate him not so much as a man but more as a servant of God in order to challenge, support, nurture, and rebuke if necessary, in order to help him develop and set goals commensurate with his abilities. I am always looking for such men. Some time ago I called out the men in the church meeting to pray for them. As they stood, I wondered why I had not felt the impact of their presence before, and then I began to think this issue through.'

Dave Bilbrough feels that secure men in the Church today are those who have a secure relationship with God, knowing that they are approved of for who they are and not for what they do. 'Just as Jesus heard the words, "This is my beloved son in whom I am well pleased" at the start of His public ministry, so security for us begins with knowing that we are loved. This comes before we actually do anything. Out of the knowledge that we are all special we have a uniqueness about us and can begin to discover what our particular gifts and abilities are.

'Then we need to be linked into a wider vision with developing relationships. Different people have been father figures to me throughout the years. They have seen my potential and have been able to see beyond my own self-made horizons. As a result I want people to know that they are loved and accepted and to know that God has a plan for them. I want to see the potential in people and give them room to make mistakes. You can see the potential in others when you know that God loves you personally.'

David Alton sees the Church in a wider context, looking at such organisations as the Jubilee Campaign, which he helped to establish, and the Movement for Christian Democracy, where he has tried to encourage both men and women to play an active role. 'Some of the people I have tried to bring on in leadership roles are certainly "secure" people, both in their faith and in their understanding of life. But people can easily get derailed. We all need mutual support, pastoral care and ministry, especially if we function in high pressure positions.'

Gerald Coates feels that to facilitate men we need to listen to them and get them to talk, not about what they are doing or what they own, but about who they are and what their dreams are. 'They need a forum where aspirations can be lived out, either in function or in friendship. This may be in public, such as in leadership or ministry. Anyone with clear life goals and ministries needs a listening ear and a forum to reassess where they are going, what they are achieving and whether their strategy is fruit-
ful.

'Many men are insecure because they feel they cannot do anything and others can do better, so why should they bother? They need to know what their sphere is, so that they can be helped to understand their own significance, skills and abilities. Other men cannot wait to get on with things and go far beyond their sphere, creating chaos as they move beyond their faith. They need to be brought back. Fellowship is the key.'

Roger Forster is aware that Western culture, through the Renaissance, has promoted the rational as opposed to the intuitive, although this is beginning to be reversed at the end of the twentieth century. He elucidates how this has played into the hands of men.

'The natural inclination and bias has been towards a rational male approach and there has been a male dominance in schools and education. Despite the example of Jesus, womankind has remained in second place and has been disadvantaged in opportunities because of the expected role of females in society. Women, for example, were not getting degrees at Cambridge until this century.

'Things are now changing and males have tried to find their superiority again in macho images, which reflect their sexuality. This has lent itself to their being total failures in every other realm because they are forever wanting to assert their masculinity through their maleness and sexuality. Hence we have the permissive society, which promotes their male philosophy. The situational ethic then develops which opens the door to relativity and therefore permissiveness.

'Here again women are disadvantaged, having either to raise the children or, more lately in being able to have an abortion. The related men have lost what it means to be a truly devoted, consistent and faithful for life lover, satisfying one woman. They also tend to abandon their children, losing their fatherhood, which is an aspect of God they were meant to carry. So many twentieth century men do not understand what manhood is, in the new ethos they have created.

'We at Ichthus firstly facilitate men in the Church with life goals and ministries and we start with clear and straightforward church discipline.

When men unacceptably (although forgivably) deviate from being faithful to their partners, the whole thing is made public. Our men know that if they step out of line in any way in sexual morals, people are going to know it and they will not have another place with us. So they have to find out how to relate to women properly instead of relating to them as sex objects.

'Secondly, we teach men to work alongside women as equals. They learn to work under women who have responsibility in different areas in the Church. They learn not to feel insecure. For those who are ministering amongst us, our pre- and post-marital counselling is structured on the male and female issues and how to understand one another.'

Men as much as women need to know they have value. Help in finding out God's meaning and purpose for their lives will give a sense of identity. Being encouraged within the Church to develop godly characters, and role modelling those who have gone before, can provide stepping stones to growth and maturity.

A key factor is learning on the job with men who can affirm and encourage. Jesus understood this well. However, we need clear objectives and God-given goals, which the Holy Spirit can bring to pass in order not to repeat the mistakes of the past, whereby big ambitions with little strategy have left the Church paying a heavy price. Learning that we do not have to compete with the opposite sex to prove a point means that meaningful partnerships can function.

Dave Tomlinson underlines for us that he sees security in men as deeply linked with their relationship with women. 'Men have a deep feeling of threat from women. I see this as more fear than hatred, although there is a fear that borders on terror with a violent reaction caused in many men. We are all different personalities and express our feelings in different ways. For example, in some people anger expresses itself as depression in an inward rather than outward way. This particular fear of women can be expressed in many ways, from violence through to the humorous put-downs, which would be more the sort of thing that I would do.

'Fear of women is a fundamental issue in men's personalities and psyches. I do not think men can find security as individuals apart from being part of a process which begins to resolve this issue of fear or terror of women. Security for men is tied up with finding an equal partnership in which they can work co-operatively and complementarily.

'Many other solutions put forward in the past, such as the need for men to have clear goals in life, are part of a masculine-orientated system. Women need to be as clear as men about goals in

their lives if we deem those things important.
Much of men's goal setting relates to the male
desire to be in control of themselves, other people
and the future. This is no longer such a high pri-
ority for me.'

R. T. Kendall comes at it from a different position.
'Here, in Westminster Chapel, there has always
been male leadership and it is a matter of finding
out the Lord's will as to which men should fulfil
which ministry. I do not think I have to lead men
into anything and I am not aware that I have any
problem in this area although may be I do have a
problem and do not know it! We have a class for
nurturing new Christians, but that is open to both
men and women.'

Tony Higton explains that in his church they
facilitate secure men in the church by challenging
them to take on leadership alongside the women.
'We are also serious about the discernment of gifts
and ministries in people and this in itself is affirming. We have a practical system for discerning
people's gifts and all our leaders have some form
of counselling even if they do not have any great
sense of need. It helps them to understand themselves. Our attitude towards women in the church
is such that we are totally committed to them
using their gifts to the full, and the men gladly
accept this. As a result it would be difficult for

a male chauvinist to be a member of this church.'

Charles Whitehead works within his church in two contexts. He explains, 'One is a Roman Catholic context and the other is a mixture of many Christian traditions. In the Catholic context we have the ordained male priesthood. This can produce too much security in the priests, and the issue becomes that of helping lay people, as a whole, to assume responsibility and ministry rather than particularly to help men alone to do so.

'The issue is very much the relationship between the lay people and the ordained clergy in leadership and ministry in the church. Many priests today were formed and trained in the fifties and sixties, when there were not a lot of offical church positions for lay people. Today's new priests are now in a Church where there is a recognised ministry and position for lay people according to the particular gift they have.

'We work hard to prepare and form young lay leaders, both men and women. We run teaching weekends and courses on the importance of having a vision for your life, hearing from God, knowing what He has called you to do and then exercising your ministry. The teaching is quite easy to do, but the second more practical side can be more difficult, depending on the local situation.

'In the Catholic Church today, many young people have been leaving the church. If their faith is nominal and they are not encouraged and given the responsibility of playing a part, they drift away. Ministry of young people to young people is a crucial factor here and essential for encouraging them to play an active part.'

Steve Chalke concludes for us. 'The traditional denominations have not been good at facilitating secure men with clear life goals and ministries. One factor in the New Churches is that they have tended to give people the opportunity to use gifts and establish ministries. When you have an aggressive church planting policy, it is all hands on deck. If, however, your kind of church is maintenance orientated, you have no need of this and leadership is static.

'My friend is at the top of a multi-national company. One day he told me that he had taken a helicopter to the airport, flown Concorde to America, done a day's work in Washington D.C., flown back and arrived home midway through the evening. His only job in the local church, which he attends every weekend, is to give out the hymn books one Sunday a month. This shows our poor policies for validating goals and ministries for men.

'In our church we actively look for people's gifts and ministries. We are just planting another church locally. Our church has a set of goals in this, which are constantly reviewed and updated. Therefore this creates targets and mobilises the ministries of our people.'

In conclusion it would seem that there are two facets or threads in this issue of men becoming secure which need to be focused upon, and both are related to the two genders. Firstly, there is the issue of male validation. Every man has a warrior heart and our best example is Jesus, who knew how to contain and enact such a life, without self-destruction. Men who follow Him, place their lives on the line.

Within the Church, men who have made that commitment need to learn more from other affirming men in order to find out who they are and what gifts lie within their personalities. Thus they can also learn how to become husbands and fathers in the way that God intended.

This leads to a second issue. It would appear that a man cannot fully be a man, until he has learned to have meaningful relationships with women, in which he does not just look at the female gender issue as a sexual one. This starts in the home, where women are usually making decisions in the lives of the next generation. Today this so often happens with fathers absent, replaced by social institutions. Boys raised with absent or weak fathers have a view of women which often needs adjustment in adulthood.

Humanism has replaced the authority of Scripture. This aids the philosophy that reason is masculine and intuition and feelings are feminine. Men can therefore easily think to relate to their women in an uninvolved logical way except in sexual matters. They also often relate in this way to their daughters when around, giving them just enough affection to prevent them going elsewhere for that affection, thinking of emotion as being just an interruption to logic, rather than as a part of whole truth.

Men who have first learned fear of women at home need to be revolutionised in their relationship to fathers. Jesus had an intimacy and trust of His Father, which affected everything He did. It made Him a warm and caring role model for us all. He was never distant. Having faced their fears and learned new ways within a committed community of believers, men who pattern themselves after Him can become intimate husbands and fathers, nurturing a new generation into well-being.

CHAPTER EIGHT

Overcoming Deception and Passivity

OUR CULTURE TODAY is in great part a product of our history. This culture inevitably infiltrates the Church. History comprises periods of reaction to previous years, and Goethe was reacting to the rationalism of the eighteenth century, with the whole romantic movement rising to its height of being. In the quote on unbridled activism he was trying to find philosophical answers to the nature of being a man and a woman.

Male chauvinism and female passivity are nothing new, neither is male passivity where chauvinism has been subverted in a personality, nor is male deception which can come forth from both. Yet in addressing these issues of weakness in men, what are the steps to be taken in order that a man can come through to maturity and marry a wife with whom he is able to establish a lifelong commitment, and at a later stage still think of extremely highly? And finally, what steps does a man need to take to father children well?

Steve Chalke begins for us with his belief that he does not think that male chauvinism has been an issue in his local church, nor has there been an issue of passivity and deception. 'The new start we had four years ago makes us a very young work. We are in the inner city, and to be honest I feel that male chauvinism is a middle-class church luxury which we cannot afford. It may be found out in the community but here in the church it really is all hands on deck.

'We have a strong leadership team, made up of both male and female. We have women leading worship as well as men, and I would not even know the ratio, because it is not an issue. We are also diverse in our opinions. For example, some of our leaders are into the Charismatic Conferences and others the Reformed Evangelical Movement. This makes life interesting but probably means that we are not so open to deception as we might otherwise be. We do not swallow everything that everybody says.'

In dealing with male chauvinism, when looking at the Catholic Church, **Charles Whitehead** sees the issue as complicated by the fact that the ordained priest is male. He explains, 'On the female side, there are a lot of orders of women and nuns who have their own authority structure. They have congregations where there are some formidably strong leaders amongst the women. With the ordained priestly ministry, however, there is within some, but certainly not all, of the priests a very chauvinistic approach. The place of women has been viewed as inferior in the church and this is now gradually being overcome. Today's training does not allow that attitude to develop, as it is no longer acceptable.

'As far as deception among men goes, I know of several cases in the sexual area. I know of leaders teaching and exercising ministry and yet being involved in quite serious sexual sin. This often seems to be linked to the exercise of power. I rely on my wife Sue to pick up fairly quickly when something is wrong and I find her intuition is usually right in these cases.

'Within the charismatic renewal in the Catholic Church, we have as many women leaders as men. However, in the top levels of leadership commmunities often do not have women in leadership, because there is still some teaching about male headship. This is beginning to change now. Elsewhere, ecumenically speaking, when meeting with other groups, we may field a team of two men and two women leaders, but there may not be another woman leader from the other evangelical denominations. I have actually been taken to one side and had it suggested that it might be better to bring just male leaders!

'As far as male passivity is concerned, I can only relate this to dealings with some of the younger leaders. They have been unable to allow their gifts and ministries to be released because of deep insecurity, which has seemed sometimes to go back to a very dominant mother or father. This can produce a highly gifted but passive child. If placed in any group with a woman who speaks her mind, such a one just retires into his shell. We had a young man where the problem was a dominant father which produced the same result. He was a gifted young man who was too frightened to be anything other than be habitually passive. We had to repair his image, linking it to his past relationship with his father, to the point where he could be free.

'Passivity, I see as relating more to general relationships and character, than to one sex or the other. I do not see it as gender related, because in another scenario a dominant father could well produce a chauvinistic son. In other parts of the world things are different. In Italy the men tend to be very chauvinistic. In Scotland recently I noticed a father and son who did nothing in the home, whilst the mother rushed around getting the meal, and then doing the washing up and the clearing away.'

David Alton's family has to be ecumenical. He explains, 'My wife is the daughter and granddaughter of Anglican clergymen. Her brother is involved in a house church. Her sister is a deacon married to a vicar and my background is Roman Catholic. I contribute weekly to columns for the Catholic newspapers but also take part at a local Anglican Church in prayer groups, and in speaking to groups on a whole range of issues. I am also a trustee or patron of a number of charities. In all these roles and in my role as a church member I watch with interest the emerging role of women.

'Some people confuse priesthood with ministry, which is a huge mistake. They assume that because a woman does not become the Pope or a bishop, this somehow means that women are unable to make a contribution. This is not true. When you consider, for instance, the contribution of Mother Teresa of Calcutta, you can see it is a gross misrepresentation to suggest that women's ministry is side-lined. From the time of Mary the mother of Jesus, women down the ages have made a remarkable contribution to church affairs and church life. In many Catholic churches today many of the leading roles are taken by women.

'I am not aware of a lot of deception in the Church. I meet a lot of honesty. But we are Isaiah's earthen vessels, full of flaws. We are a church of sinners, with plenty of room for more. At the evangelical Anglican church which I attend on some Sunday evenings, women there also play a strong part in running the fellowship. There is a real team effort between the minister and his wife who also teaches in one of the local schools.

Between them they seem to have the exactly right relationship with each other and decisions are taken after consultation with people in honesty and openness.'

For **R. T. Kendall** the question of overcoming male chauvinism in the Church suggests a biased standpoint that this is a deadly evil that needs to be dealt with. He explains, 'It is a matter of one's perspective. The question posed seems to reflect a great fear of male leadership, which perhaps some would call chauvinistic. I do not necessarily think it is the correct word to describe a tradition where leadership is regarded as male. I think to call it chauvinistic is like calling a socialist Marxist. You can have male leadership without being chauvinistic. This is not a problem that we have felt we needed to unmask here.

'We do not have a problem in the area of male deception. Some of the newer charismatic churches have had this problem, but we have not gone far enough down that road. Neither do we have the problem of passive men where the women are seen to be doing most of the work in relationship to church building.'

Phil Mohabir tries to deal with male chauvinism in the church at different levels by personal counselling, confrontation and getting people to have a change of mind-set, as well as altered agendas. 'I always try to put mixed teams to work together and demonstrate as fact that the love of God overcomes our natural prejudices. Active promotion of the functional role and ministry of women in the Church is another way to break through. Accepting and promoting women in their own right by recognising their gifts and giving teaching to develop their abilities are positve steps which prevent us from being just silent admirers or onlookers.

'I overcome deception in the church by teaching and by exposing people to healthy role models. We also enable people to relearn truth in groups together. Deliverance and renunciation within a discipleship forum are a third string to our bow.

'I seek to overcome passivity in the church by not putting upon the men an expectation that God does not put on them. For example, not all men are leaders. I encourage those who are leaders to be leaders and those who are followers to be followers. All need to be fulfilled and not be lazy or haphazard. Through repentance and training, men can become disciplined. It is also essential to understand that without the inner working of the Holy Spirit, we cannot reform people who are not being transformed by His power.'

Chauvinism is therefore countered in many ways from counselling to working in teams. Deception is countered by teaching and healthy role models, while passivity is countered by encouragement and repentance. Right relationships play a major part in training, care and safeguards within the church community. Placing single people with married couples and recovering homosexuals can likewise play a part in helping to deal with problems in relationships within the church. Thus people are aided to become secure and mature believers.

For **John Noble** there are two main ways in which he has sought to address male chauvinism in the Church. He explains, 'The first has been to provide working models of men and women labouring side by side in mutually submitted relationships. The second has been to create opportunities to talk and teach on the subject. Once again, wherever possible, I would try to ensure that men and women share the ministry. I have also actively encouraged women to write and have been, at least partly res-ponsible for a number of books, including Christine's *What in the World is God Saying About Women?* In addition I have sought to share at a personal level particularly with leaders. Finally, both Christine and I have worked to bring women into a place of confidence and security so that they can face this issue peacefully and prayerfully when and wherever they find it.

'Certainly deception and passivity amongst men are rife, and the difficulty is that because of the nature of our plight we do not know it and if we did we would not care. It was an obvious, but none the less masterly stroke by the enemy to play to the weaknesses of men and women as they were manifested in the Garden of Eden at the Fall. The female reaction of over-responsibility the "It's all my fault" syndrome has fuelled the fire of suspicion in men and convinced them that women are dangerous and must, therefore, be kept in their place.

'On the other hand, the male reaction of passing the buck and shelving responsibility or the, "It's nothing to do with me," attitude, confirms women in their frustration and low self-esteem. This then endorses men's belief that they are superior and leaves them free to do nothing. So the scene is set for the eternal struggle between the sexes.

'Thank God that Jesus came to break the deadlock and remove the curse, stripping Satan of his power and showing us a way into harmony once again.'

For **Roger Forster** the biological separation of male and female helps in understanding humanity as a whole, and not just the division that exists. 'The original mandate, recorded in Genesis 1:28, was for male and female to have dominion together and subdue the earth. By working and functioning together we are compensating for each other. This could mean a dominance and a passivity, which is also redressed in our developing of ourselves.

'If we say that a woman is totally one thing and the man totally another, then the only way they can relate is on a sexual level. This is the last thing we want. One man needs one woman for that, and needs to treat the rest of women as mirrors, if you like, to understand himself. Women likewise have the same need of men.'

Joel Edwards feels that men need to hear very clearly the message about accountability, particularly within the domestic setting. They need to know that accountability is not superiority. He continues, 'Within the black community, the history of dislocation of family life due to slavery, and the resulting poor male role models, have caused an acute problem in this area. Teaching is needed and men need to be confronted about their insecurities from within a secure environment. This helps everyone to see that they have a value and that they do not need to struggle with the myth of superiority. We need to know what God requires concerning our accountability as men and offer to our families and churches our strengths and gifts. We also need more positive, balanced and secure role models, and we need counselling for anyone who places undue emphasis on a particular nuance of scripture, for example, when getting the headship issue out of proportion.

'We need to know the proper interpretation of scripture in order to avoid deception. It is essential to be clear about any wrong line that is taken and how it leads us out of fellowship with the majority of worshipping believers. If we are moving against the whole tone of historical theology and accumulated orthodoxy, there needs to be some confrontation, at first privately and then publicly, if it threatens the Church and the life of the community.'

Dave Tomlinson feels that basic education in the Christian context means having better teaching on the subject of male chauvinism. He explains, 'Men and women working together is not a purely theological issue. You cannot, however, make a lot of headway without dealing with the theology. We must rethink what the Bible really does say. Goal posts need to be established.

'I have tried, when possible, to place a man in a position where he is more dependent on a woman's contribution. Putting people into teams where experience is gained often leads men to appreciate having a female boss. Team work incorporates people of widely diverse temperaments, persuasions and gender and connects them clearly to other people. This will also help stop the likelihood of deception being at work in the church.

'In many churches today leadership only reproduces its own kind and you get more of what you already have, instead of more of what you need, which is diversity. We must include men and women of different personalities and temperaments. I have seen many men getting into wrong relationships with women in the church over the years and have observed how the men have built up a whole rationale in their minds to justify what they are doing, because they have not been vulnerable and open. The antidote to deception is men and women together in community.

'Passivity is often an expression of unwillingness to take responsibility. Men, as well as having a fear of women and wanting to remain in control, also want to be very dependent on women in terms of real responsibility. This is often true in family life and they can become passive. In some situations this produces responsible matriarchal figures who never have the clear authority that goes with their role.'

Dave Bilbrough feels that the starting place in our relationship with people must be respect and affirmation. He explains, 'We have all been affected by our backgrounds. It has been said that much of the motivation behind American presidents and world leaders in their quest for power has been a looking for approval from mothers or fathers who did not affirm them in their early life. Male chauvinism is tied up with power seeking. There is always a reason why the person is looking for power, just as there is a reason for a person being passive. Today I would much more want to respect people, hearing what they are saying from a personal sense of security.

'Often male chauvinism can be seen in the music scene. We have few female worship leaders and few female singers. This is partly because we do not have the expectation they will come up with the goods and we do not make room or give time to address the subject of developing women worship leaders. In the book of Revelation, chapter twelve talks about there being singing in heaven with "Hallelujahs" and "Amen". The "Hallelujah" is the conquest that is going on, the activity of God on the march. The "Amen" means "Thy will be done." It is these two aspects coming together that make up the fabulous mystery of what is happening. Conquest on its own leads to power, with the person thinking they are all important. Saying, "Let your will be done, Lord" on its own, is passivity. These two aspects must be our praise statements as we move forward.

Often the reason behind deception, particularly heresy, is some deep hurt. Male deception is often born when we feel that we are the only ones who see something clearly. Isolationism also often plays a part, when men are less able to open themselves up to others around them. People who can be vulnerable and are willing to share new truth with others can be spared building a whole empire around a single truth, which then becomes a deception.'

'Tom Marshall, speaking at a recent conference, shared how someone who is, for example, cynical, is someone who has taken a positive attribute such as discernment and allowed it to move slightly out of control. The result is that a strength becomes a weakness. The thing that ultimately keeps us away from deception is devotion and an openness to God. If we use words to back up doctrine which is not essentially coming from our hearts, and are not vulnerable enough to believe that we might actually be wrong, we will display that superiority that precedes deception.'

Many men in the church do not have time to be passive—they are too busy and even stressed! However, some men who are highly motivated at work come home to be demotivated by confrontation with a wife and hassle with children and house. They need to be taught to give themselves strategically even when tired. Women who both work and look after children can also be demotivated. Both need to find that Godly blance in their lives of 'Let your will be done Lord.'

Male deception comes then through sins of either omission or commission. Deception is both the capacity to be deceived or something you can do to someone else. It is enhanced through isolation. When it hits a church it is often a highly intuitive person, often a woman, who will pick up that something is wrong, but with no rational basis. Also people in prayer will come up with things they do not understand, then afterwards the problem can logically start to unfold and reveal itself.

How clear a church remains, depends on how freely these gifts function at leadership level, particularly the intuitive gift of discernment so often found in a woman. It also depends on how good relationships are and whether people are walking in the light with one another. Maturity of character and gift are essential in these matters. Once disclosed, deception can be dealt with by the leadership and it can be decided who is deceived, with preventative or corrective action taking place.

Male chauvinism is in the Church and many do not see it. It can be overcome by a group of people who are treating women as equals. If this is modelled well many people can learn. When men are doing well, the endorsement of other men means a lot to them, as it does with women.

Aspects of culture give us glimpses of what God really intended. Since only women can give birth to new human beings, there is no inherent reason why they should not be valued more than men rather than less! Yet overall, it tends to be that they have less recognition in producing the new life, than the male warrior who risks his own life in the process of destroying the lives of others! If culture is the arena by which humanity tries to assert its control over nature, this explains why women, who are closer to nature than men, are valued at that level!

How the Church needs to answer these aspects of life! How the world needs to see what God intended! We need the Holy Spirit to produce working life relationships that refute the assumption that man is greater than woman or indeed woman greater than man, but rather show how they are both equal and complementary images of God.

CHAPTER NINE

Patriarchy in the Church?

STRONG PATRIARCHY CAN be said to make men complacent. Many do not want to change and hope that the structures in society will remain as they have for centuries past. They want paternalism to continue, so that their own influence is dominant.

Feminism has highlighted the stereotyping which results when men act in this way. Feminists feel such men to be beyond change and thus irrelevant. Yet it is evident that men, who are people too, cannot be considered apart from women. There exists a 'male-female' polarity, which is anchored in God Himself and cannot be denied.

We have, therefore, to address the issue of paternalism related to gender. We have to ask, not as the feminists do about its irrelevance, but rather as Christians in this generation, whether the Bible teaches patriarchy in the Church, either in New Testament times or timelessly. Having found our answers, we have then to apply the conclusions practically.

Dave Tomlinson says, 'Emphatically no, the Bible does not teach patriarchy in the Church. The confusion comes when people go to the Old Testament to establish the idea and then the concepts are "read over" into the church. Relating the historical life of Israel in this way means that you are bound to get it wrong.

'I take the view that hermaneutics should start with Jesus. We must interpret the rest of the Bible from Jesus both forwards and backwards. God meets people where they are, but does not leave them there. God introduced Himself into a nation of people who were not only patriarchal and chauvinistic but also racist and tribalistic. At times He seems to approve of these things and fits in with their tribalistic and nationalistic designs. God was then breaking into human history, but the culmination of all things is in Christ, who broke down all the barriers of race—Jew and Samaritan, of gender—men and women, and of status—slave and free.'

John Noble believes that the Bible teaches that the patriarchal system was instituted as a result of the Fall. He explains, 'In Genesis 3 verse 16 God said to the woman, "Your desire shall be for your husband and he shall rule over you." Such words had never before been uttered. Until then there was joint responsibility: the man and the woman were to rule over creation together. In Christ this curse has been dealt with and removed. Now, through humility, sacrifice, service and obedience, men and women can function together again in mutual submission to the gifts and calling God has placed within them.

'Of course, God is our Father and human fatherhood should be a reflection of the heavenly, but men are so taken up with authority that we forget that God's goal is not authority but fellowship. Authority is necessary where there is rebellion, but it is redundant when there is repentance and humility. I will always be the father of my children but my goal is friendship with them.

'The patriarchal system involved a male standing between the people and God, a husband for his wife, a father for his children, a priest for the people and so on. In Christ this was blown away. Now every individual has direct access to the Father and His throne, in this respect there is neither male nor female. As you know, David Pawson is a personal friend and I deeply respect his wisdom in certain areas. However in this matter it seems to me he borders on heresy. In his book *Leadership is Male*, he implies in a number of places that women relate to God through men and just as men are to be subordinate to God, so women are to be subordinate to men.

'The problem is that David does not differentiate between sexuality and masculinity/ feminity, and he confuses the two. Sexuality pictures the future relationship of Christ with the Church. It is a shadow and will fade in the light of the reality. On the other hand masculinity and feminity are a reflection of the very image of God and they are here to stay. This thinking sows seeds of doubt that a woman can indeed meet with God on equal terms via the cross. Throughout church history it has led to the subjugation and oppression of women.

'On the back of David's book there is a diagram which deeply concerns me. Diagrams can be helpful but God didn't inspire any of His prophets to draw diagrams. Theology might have been much simpler if he had. The diagram shows us that women can only relate to God through men until they get their resurrection bodies, when presumably the human bits that identify our sexuality will have dropped off or been removed. This puts our relationship with the Lord on purely sexual terms, which is very dangerous. Apart from the damage to married women it puts an extremely unhealthy pressure on single women. Apparently there is no place for them in David's thinking and they are bound to feel that in order to have any kind of ministry at all they should be married. This is clearly not scriptural as Paul urged us all to be single as he was.'

R. T. Kendall says, 'As far as I understand it, the position that David Pawson exposes I am somewhat sympathetic with. I cannot elaborate because I have not read the book carefully, nor have I read the answers to it. I would not be against a woman speaking. We had Jackie Pullinger speaking one Sunday night. She is an extraordinary woman. So we cannot be cast in the mould that David Pawson would be in, as I think he would not have a Jackie Pullinger speaking as we did, but I do not definitely know that this is the case. There is no doubt that women prophesy, but these issues are not black and white.'

Joel Edwards expresses that for him a patriarchal attitude in the church leads to paternalism. 'I believe in genuine equal opportunities. If Galatians 3:28 means anything, it means the potential for total equality before God in ministry, with a clear system of accountability. In church terms I see a spiritual house, built up for the glory of God, in which we are growing as per gifts rather than as per gender.'

Steve Chalke feels that on the issue of whether the Bible teaches patriarchy in the Church, the truth is schizophrenic. He explains, 'In Britain, we have a missionary history where it is OK for women to go off to Africa to preach, teach and lead, but back at home it is a different story. Pragmatically, if women had not served as missionaries, who would have done? The men who tend to be very passive sit back and pontificate about doctrine and the rights and wrongs of women in ministry. I have to ask again—is it all a middle class luxury, where we can afford to fight over the small things instead of tackling the main issues?

'The women in ministry issue has been most fiercely fought in the larger middle-class provincial town churches. From my perspective, within the New Testament, there does not appear to be one clear line of teaching about the role of a woman in leadership. For instance Paul, on close inspection, seems to be saying different things to different churches. We are looking at the New Testament for something it does not say. Paul wrote a set of letters to different situations dealing with different local issues. To understand his letters we need to understand each specific situation and set of issues. To draw out a universal principle from such writing, making it apply to every situation, is probably going further than the New Testament itself goes.

'I preached in a Brethren Assembly where all the ladies were issued with head coverings. As I started to speak I noticed a girl right in front of me wearing a skimpy top and a skirt slit up to her backside. She had on a head covering but I have never struggled so much to concentrate on an introduction to the first worship song. The Assembly had kept the letter of the law, but had totally lost sight of what Paul was really saying to his audience in Corinth.'

The Church is referred to as the Body of Christ, which is male and it is also referred to as the Bride of Christ which is female. There is equality in these teachings. The whole subject of Christian personalism can hardly be considered apart from the charisma of womanhood. The generally male prophetic writing of the Old Testament points towards the incarnation through a female. It is the virgin Mary who becomes the prototype of faith. In her, faith becomes certain. As in Hebrew liturgy the patriarchs, Abraham, Isaac and Jacob are invoked, so within whole sections of Christendom Mary is revered. This intertwining of the female and male is a vibrant statement on its own.

Tony Higton shares: 'From the teaching of the scripture (e.g. 1 Corinthians 11:3) I believe that the overall presiding role in the church should be male. This does not mean that women cannot be in eldership, I believe they can. We had an all-male eldership some years ago but I realised that we were suffering from not having the insights of some of the leading women. We would now include women, and particularly the wives of male elders, assuming they have spiritual maturity.

'So often male elders make high-powered

decisions one week, then come together the following week having changed their minds. They have discussed matters with their wives! We short-circuit all of that by having wives there in the first place! If man is incomplete without woman, can leadership be complete if it excludes women? To have an all-male leadership without female input is not the ideal that God intends.

'In some way I would like to be in favour of women Priests, because I feel so strongly about women's issues, and in fact I do not oppose the ordination of women. However, theologically, I still have a problem in this area because I do not see the New Testament allowing a woman to be in headship, which ordination inevitably means in the Church of England. However, even in Scripture, there are exceptions. Women do take headship positions. So it does not appear to be an absolute rule for all circumstances.'

Gerald Coates feels that there is truth in the fact that the patriarchal society we live in is a reflection of divine fatherhood and that Jesus was and needed to be a man and not a woman. He explains, 'Had he been a woman he would not have had a hearing 2000 years ago. However, there are plenty of feminine expressions of the godhead in scripture including Jesus talking about Himself being like a mother hen wanting to gather her chicks. Similarly the twelve disciples were all men and gained a hearing, and must replace the twelve tribes of Israel.

'Jesus was not sexist and He enabled these men to do what only they could do in that culture. However, there were many women around Him, who were not put down by Him. There is biblical emphasis that leans towards the fact that patriarchal society is a reflection of divine fatherhood, but that is not to the point of exclusivity. Women were not excluded from ministry, prophecy, leadership or politics in the Bible.

'The high-class business lady of Proverbs 31 is an interesting entrepeneur. You cannot divide life into sacred and secular, and where a woman may be overseeing the lives of many people in the secular world, she cannot be excluded from being a housegroup leader in the Church! Women make just as good managers as men, sometimes better, and that is true in the church also.'

Phil Mohabir has a problem here, not feeling that leadership is male, yet believing that there is a kind of patriarchy taught in the Bible emphasising fatherhood to the nation. He continues, 'In that sense the Bible does teach that there should be fatherhood in the community and fathers who teach, train and nurture their children and are themselves role models for their children. They are prophets to their own household. I feel, however, that too many men, including Christian men, leave that role to be filled by the mother or the teachers in school.

'I do not know enough theologically to make a proper comment on this controversy. I listen to both sides and am not convinced that either have got it right. I believe that there is something else in the heart of God, which we have not yet discovered concerning the male–female partnership. These current arguments create a divisive competitive spirit rather than encouraging the partnership which I believe was God's original intention between male and female. God wants us working together for the good of society in a harmonious and meaningful way, putting our strengths together and covering each other's weaknesses. This is a true reflection of the heart of God. The authority issue is clouding God's eternal purpose and His original intention for the male–female relationship.'

Roger Forster explains his position. 'My own understanding of even the assumed patriarchy of Abraham is somewhat conditioned by my understanding of the way that Sarah was presented in Scripture. God changes her from being *my* princess to *the* princess. Obviously proprietorial rights have been lessened in Abraham—she belongs first to God not to him. Secondly, the only time she called Abraham "Lord" was in connection with going to bed and having a child when she thought she was beyond it. She said, "Shall I have pleasure of my lord?" On another occasion God says to Abraham not that he should make her obey him, but rather he was to "harken" (which is a form of the same word as "obey") to Sarah and do what she said. Therefore any idea of patriarchy meaning ignoring the authority on the place of the woman is incorrect.

'The Jews had certainly moved on into such problems that by the time of Jesus the biblical Old Testament position of a woman had basically been lost and a woman's lot had deteriorated. This demonstrates that there are other elements in the history of the Bible which are not meant to be taken as divine injunctions on revelation. They are obviously incorporated from societies round about.

'If a society is in any way going to retain the idea of a continuing seed right from the word go, such as for example, 'the seed of woman would crush the serpent's head', then there is a sense in which God or someone has to choose how that seed can be traced. You cannot have both a matriarchy and a patriarchy at the same time in order to record the seed. God, it seems, did choose patriarchy and it may be that it reflected His fatherhood, but we see no statement at all that it does. It seems gratuitious to assume so. It seems a rather pragmatic solution in order to see that the promise has been fulfilled by tracing the seed through the father rather than the mother, which would have been more difficult in a polygamous society. It is also pragmatic in that most, although not all, other societies around would be doing the same.

'In the New Testament, there are also other reasons for Jesus choosing twelve men. For example pragmatically, He knew males would dominate the next two thousand years. However, Jesus wanted to challenge the order of the twelve tribes of Israel by setting up a new Israel. Because the twelve tribes were based on a patriarchy of literal fathers, Jesus set up the twelve apostles as spiritual fathers of the new humanity.

'From then on others also come in such as Junia (a woman) and Paul, however the first twelve were symbols and in this there is no necessity for any male hierarchy to be perpetuated in the ongoing apostolate. The Bible does not teach patriarchy in the Church. It may infer it perhaps, but to say that it does is almost a provocative statement. It is like saying that the Bible teaches that every time the Holy Spirit comes upon someone, they speak in tongues. You might infer that, but you cannot teach it from scripture.'

Charles Whitehead sees patriarchy as clearly defined in the Old Testament, but does not see it as being continued into the New Testament. He concludes, 'I see the New Covenant as being different. I am speaking from a slightly difficult position, because in the Catholic Church we do stick to the ordained male ministry. I do not find clear teaching that this is a model of church which should reflect into society.

'Taking the priestly ministry, it is not that the priest is in some way superior to the people, it is just that he has a different calling and task. Priesthood and laity are totally equal before God in every sense of the word, but the one has a particular calling that he is following and the other has different callings. This is much more the model that I see coming through the New Testament today. We are all different and it is not a case of being more or less authoritarian.

'The cultural context of the New Testament is also important. Paul gives us various pictures of the impact of the Church on different levels of society. It is quite clear that there were a number of wealthy women supporting the disciples in the early church. During the first three or four centuries, the position of deaconess was very important. When new converts were brought to church or baptised, deacons baptised men and deaconesses baptised women, before they were all brought through to where the elders laid hands on them. Some of our reverend mothers are the most powerful and respected to voices of today. They are sometimes even more powerful than the priests!'

The Bible teaches much about God's omnipotence and Jesus addresses God as 'Father'. Our relationship with our father is as important as that with our mother. It is a great mistake to confuse it with an intolerant disposition towards women or to confuse it with the unnecessary suppression of women and their rights. These two things are very different from our relationship with God as Father!

Men who become loving men, in the Christian sense, deal with the issue of patriarchy and make it cease to be an unjust institution. They do this without losing the essence of the father heart of God. Somehow we need to raise a new standard of what it means to be a Christian man or woman totally committed to Christ and mutuality amongst His people. Teams of such humanity will touch people and places not yet reached with the gospel.

MEN IN RELATIONSHIP TO WOMEN

CHAPTER TEN

Insecurity and the Cultural Fear of Women

MANY THINGS WHICH are said and done today, assume a cultural atmosphere of fear of women. This was not always so. Archaeologists have pointed to widespread evidence of a matrilocalor female led basis of society in history, in various parts of the world. Margaret Ehrenberg in her conclusion of *Women in Pre-History* decides that throughout human history the great majority of women who have ever lived, had far more status than women of recent times and they probably had equality with men too on a life-functioning basis.

It is interesting to track through Scriptures and see history from a biblical perspective. God changed Sarah's name to show that her links to Him superseded those to Abraham. There is also a suggestion of 'female ruler' in her new name of 'anointed one'. At one point Abraham was told to obey her, in Genesis 21:12, with reference to Hagar's removal from the family. Isaac took Rebekah his new wife into his mother's tent, after she had been given a free choice concerning marrying him. He, it seems, was far less consulted than Rebekah's mother and brother!

Strong women today are often feared by men, yet Boaz says of Ruth that she is a woman of strength and power. The woman of Proverbs 31:10 can be translated in the scriptures as, 'a masculine woman who can find?' In another text, the Syrial translation says 'a strong, powerful and virile woman'. Such women are hardly weak women who will be easily led astray!

Today many men are intimidated by a growing host of strong women and the term 'female chauvinism' is now being used. Something has happened amongst women, and this has highlighted the fact that many men do not know who they are, they only know what they do, what they own and who they know.

Threatened men can become remote, as their fathers often were before them. They can become passive in the face of responsibility. Occasionally violence breaks out, when they feel powerless and their feelings of inadequacy lead to abdication of their fatherhood roles. Another type of man will fantasise about women and yet be afraid of them. This at worst moves into a wrong kind of dependency, which the pop world sings about in its songs which declare 'can't live without you baby,' and the love relationship becomes an idol.

Society compensates and frequently over-evaluates male achievement, while it debases the values of womanhood, and even motherhood itself. Women begin to ape men uneasily out of envy and resentment. The flight from the feminine is far more widespread today than at other times in history. For the woman, her femininity can become a deprivation and a negative thing. She then too perpetuates the *status quo*.

We thus precondition our children. How they learn to talk depends on the community language to which they are exposed during the early months. In this issue they either hear that we are sexually equal or they hear that there is a war on! How do we address these insecurities? Are women inferior to men? What does God intend for us in our male female relationships?

Phil Mohabir shares his thoughts. 'How can I answer this question because I am not an Englishman! I feel that the statement "an Englishman's home is his castle" is not biblical, because it gives an impression of the man ruling supreme with a rod of iron! It also gives an impression that nobody is welcome. People are to keep out, and be locked out, because the home is exclusively one man's possession. The Bible does not teach exclusivity but it does teach privacy.

'I believe in the family unit and also in extended families. Within the husband–wife relationship I want partnership, because I feel that this is really God's heart. Paul's teaching emphasises that a man must accept responsibility for his family, and take the lead in it. This must not be at the expense of the wife's contribution. Rather the husband must bring out what is best in his wife, in order to create the kind of atmosphere where everyone is secure and can develop and grow to their full potential.

'As far as submission is concerned, I feel that the Bible does teach that in deadlock situations the Lord will hold the husband responsible for the choices and decisions he makes for his family. If there is disagreement the wife should voluntarily submit, knowing that her husband must give an account to the Lord. She can pray, seek help, dialogue and even protest and register her disapproval, but she must allow him to make a decision for which he must give account. This does not mean that she must not disagree nor be consulted. The nature of submission does not preclude these things. She has the right to disagree and must not be made to submit against her will. Where there is true love and care, the home need not become a battlefield. We must not manipulate, blackmail, impose our will on each other and certainly we should not expect anyone to submit to the other if their conscience is violated. A generous dose of sweet reasonableness goes a long way to maintain harmony.

'I too have been affected by these issues and am

a product of our environment. I have had to allow the Holy Spirit and the Word of God to recondition my mind. I do not want to be just a product of our cultural environment, but I want to be a child of God in every respect. If that means repenting of some of my cultural or natural traits then so help me God. In my culture, where I grew up, there was a fear of men amongst the women. Here in the West I notice that there is a fear of female domination and a lot of men are in reaction.

'As Christians we must get back to the Word of God and seek to live in obedience to it. I have lived in two cultures seeing both the good and the bad in both. I want to make it clear that I feel women have had a raw deal in our cultures and we still have not got it right. Christian men in particular have a very long way to go to develop and bring out the best in women. We are robbing the Church of more than sixty to seventy per cent of our resources. Women need to be forthcoming and make use of their opportunities. Men need to make space but women must not be reluctant to fill that space—"Take your rightful place, sisters".'

Gerald Coates is clear that women are not inferior to men. He explains, 'To say this would be unbiblical. God wants harmony and partnership between men and women. There are skills and abilities that my wife Anona has that I don't and vice versa. Most of these have nothing to do with gender. In order for us to function in our household with budget, children and social life, I need to recognise that the person I am married to does have skills I don't possess and needs to be listened to. This also applies the other way round. The most successful partnerships are those based on agreed expectations and where they can be shaped change occurs. When our functions change our abilities evolve and this too creates a harmony.'

John Noble feels that this issue is not just a British problem but it is worldwide and exists in all cultures. He says 'The truth of it can be seen in one simple statistic. Women do 66 per cent of all the world's work and earn only 10 per cent of its income (and incidentally only own 1 per cent of its property). My guess is that it is the women who do little work in terms of daily grind, such as queens and film stars, who actually earn the 10 per cent. In my experience the women who really work 18 hours a day in third world situations get nothing or very little for all that they do.

'Looking at women in world terms, not only are they not inferior, they are infinitely superior! In most countries they quietly bear the brunt and pain of surviving, whilst they feed and bring up their families. They grow the food and harvest it, they feed the animals as well as keep the home and often this is done against the background of male abuse and brutality or at least negligence.

'If they are so open to deception and Satanic manipulation, I cannnot imagine why they have not conducted a major revolt against man and his violent ways! It is man who has been responsible for the invention and production of weapons of mass destruction. It is man who has amassed huge fortunes whilst his fellows starve. It is man who has sought to displace God and rule the world alone. In purely human terms, on the evidence available, women should be counted superior every time. No wonder the one promise made in the garden, was given to a woman. I doubt God could have trusted a man to say 'Be it unto me according to your will' as Mary did.

'Thank God in Christ men are included, but we do not deserve it. I have absolutely no doubt that what God intended was for Adam and Eve to rule His creation jointly and through obedience, eat of the tree of life and receive immortality. Their sexual or marriage relationship was intended to reflect the future marriage of Christ as the bridegroom, we all being the bride. Human sexuality is but a shadow that will fade into insignificance in the light of the ultimate relationship of Jesus and the Church.'

Roger Forster continues with this theme of the Garden of Eden. 'Firstly, Adam and Eve were meant to function and have dominion together, not one to have dominion over the other. Dominion was never given within the relationships of human beings, it was given over everything else. The authority given to the apostles was that they should preach the gospel, cast out demons and heal the sick. This is not authority over a church or people's relationships. I do not mind having authority taken over the devil, but I do have a problem with the use of church authority and canon rule and law if we talk in hierarchical terms.

'Ordination, meaning ranking or the hierarchy of a career ladder, is causing many problems. We have come to this issue the wrong way around. Males tend to be terribly bureaucratic and the more this dominates, the more women are marginalised until the issue breaks out again. Women are often uninterested in ordination, while men see this career ladder as their way of getting some power. However, power in the Church was meant to be power over the enemy and over sin, and the power to preach good news and to cast out demons.

'Secondly, in the first century there is an unanswerable case for the idea of headship being almost exclusively a source. Adam and Eve's relationship in Genesis 2 was always based on the male–female relationship and never on authority. The idea of head being authoritative as opposed to being a source, such as the head of a river, has not yet been justified. Tertullian in his day in the third century had to justify, in his introduction to the subject, the idea that headship hardly ever had authority connotations, but that in the case of men and women he felt it did.

'Even if there were authority implied in some cases in the New Testament or first-century Greek, Genesis 2 does not say that this is what the text means. Adam, being the head, had Eve taken out of him, which means he was her source and nothing else. If there is any idea of authority, it is only in the fact that the head of a river determines which way the river will flow. Until contraception, a woman would be having child after child in years gone by and it was necessary for there to be a source and a protection for the family life. Nature teaches no more than this. It does not teach that it is for the woman to be bossed about! Women are not inferior to men. Genesis 1 shows development from the inferior animal creatures of creation up to man and woman. Woman is the last in the line and woman therefore would logically be, if anything superior!'"

R. T. Kendall shares his thoughts. 'God said that it was not good for man to be alone. It is interesting that in man's pre-fallen state he needed to have fellowship with someone else. It is not enough that we have God alone in our life. We need companionship. Woman therefore was made for the man, but she is in no way inferior.'

Each of us is unique and made in the image of God. The fact that we are men or women does not make us greater or lesser in God's sight. We are all equally important. Those who try to place a burden of guilt on women and put them in an inferior position are misrepresenting God's plan for each person. In the growth of Puritanism more and more women were denied rights or privileges and were in some places held as the greater source of sin, by which was meant the gratification of sexual desire.

God, however, intended Adam and Eve to live in perfect harmony in accordance with His plans. The great deceiver destroyed that. People place too much emphasis on Eve's initial deception. Adam was also deceived, being quite prepared to take part in the deception. He was not morally superior to Eve. We are all fallen, whether women or men.

The Christian believes that there is only one way for either a man or a woman to be remade. That is to come to a loving understanding of God through His son Jesus. New life requires an acceptance of Christ, who brings new life to birth. Christ the new Adam has put right what the first Adam destroyed. Guilt and blame can stop.

Joel Edwards sees Adam and Eve's complementary behaviour primarily in roles and functions rather than a competition between them. 'I see different roles and I do not have a problem with authority and submission. I believe it is to be found firstly within the domestic context of accountability, where the man is not the boss but the servant of the family.

'There is a legitimate feminism within the context of our church life. It must not come out of a secular humanistic mind-set. Young women often challenge the status quo legitimately, but come from a secular mind-set not actually grappling with the scriptures. We must not start from the wrong place, asking the right question, otherwise we will end up in the wrong place with the wrong answers or even sometimes the right answers in the wrong place.

'We may sometimes have a very strong woman who has an effect on her husband and sons. The question I then ask is this: to what extent has the woman always been a strong person? Then I need to ask: to what extent did she have to become a strong person in order to occupy a vacant position? This can be hard to tell, without tracing the roots. I know of a church leadership situation, where a woman was so strong that the church asked for a man to lead them after she left. I believe this was a result of the latent fear of women within people, which is even sometimes found in women. It can also be an irrational response to the gender issue, which is to see that certain behaviour, such as assertive conduct, does not in some people's opinions belong to the female domain!'

A friend of **Steve Chalke** recently said to him that he felt that Steve was not hindered by the kind of fears that he felt had held him down personally, coming from his childhood. Steve feels grateful for the stability of his upbringing and the good models that his mum and dad provided. 'My parents argued quite a lot. Both openly expressed their opinions in a healthy way. My dad was a very strong person but no stronger than my mother. Their relationship was one of two equals. They were different but equal. In fact my mother is probably one of the strongest people I have ever met yet she is not aggressive.

'My dad, who is Anglo-Indian, came from a culture where women were expected to be the workhorses. My mum has always just got on with things. She has initiative and was the central figure in our home. My parents are committed Christians. They never congratulated us much yet I never felt put down by them. I was taught how to relate to people well and the whole male–female issue has never really been an issue to me. I think that my upbringing helped me to see men and women as equals.

'I often ask my team in Oasis to tell me if I am sexist at all so that I can deal with it. Adam and Eve were meant to complement each other. In

Ecclesiastes 3 it is written that a threefold cord is very strong. Teamwork makes for strength. Although I am perceived as the boss of Oasis, in reality there are four of us who lead the work. I would never dream of overriding what the others said because I founded Oasis, because I know that the day I do that, they would walk out of the door, probably not physically, but in terms of their ownership and some of their commitment.

'I went into marriage thinking I loved my wife, which I did, but the love I love her with now is completely different, not fainter, but a million times deeper. I lean on her and need her and cannot fully function without her. I could not supply her job description—it is imperceptible how she complements me as I am. She too needs me and together we are so much stronger. There are also several women that I know very well and I have close relationships with them. My wife is not threatened by this, she knows them well—and she would tell me if she was uncomfortable. I am not aware that in any of these relationships there is any measure of control.'

Charles Whitehead has not felt any sense of insecurity or fear of women, their position or their role. 'I have never seen them as inferior or superior to men and I believe that what God intended for Adam and Eve was a partnership. I think Adam and Eve had different roles and gifts but were never the less equal together.

'The place of women in any of the groups that I am involved in has been simply a question of gifting and skills with the personalities, doing what God is calling them to do. I have no problem, where leadership is concerned, involving authority of a woman over other men, provided I feel that the woman is gifted to do that.

'Our Friday night prayer meeting has a leadership team which takes pastoral care of people and also plans any teaching. It is made up of half women and half men and we share all the leadership equally. We have one woman who is extremely good at confrontation in a positive way, when it needs to be done whether with men or women. Another woman is very much better at the more gentle kind of pastoral work. We just need to recognise the gifts in everyone.

'At the moment one of my concern is the way that a lot of young teenage boys speak of women. I find the growth of bad attitudes and words quite appalling and the increase in pornography and rape has links with this. There is a disrespect for the person, even to the point of hatred. It may be that these things need to come out and become worse in order to be addressed.'

Dave Bilbrough feels that God created 'man', which means humanity or mankind, and that out of mankind came male and female. 'I see partnership in this, with God's original intention being that Adam and Eve should work together to rule over the earth. Woman was not meant to drag behind the man and be inferior, but rather with her different facets and abilities she should complement him.

'In the recent past of the house church movement there was much emphasis on women submitting to men and men always being right. This was often sourced in insecurity, although there were good intentions behind the teaching of releasing men from passivity and getting them mobilised, instead of always allowing the women to lead. There were some damaging effects on women as a result and the suppression made them feel less valuable.

'We are all called to be submissive people. I aspire to being submissive to people who have gifts and who function in the areas of their gift. My wife will acknowledge that I am better in certain spheres than she is and I know that in others she is better than I. At the end of the day, in a home, a man and a woman should talk things through together and come to a good decision. My wife might recognise that I have a more considered and wider overview, whilst she reacts more quickly.'

Tony Higton concludes this section. 'Any exercise of authority should be liberating to those affected by it. If it is not, something is seriously wrong. I question how much fear of women there is in society. Certainly some men are seriously threatened by women. My views of authority and submission are based on years of biblical study and critical thought, not on psychological hang-ups. There is no inequality between men and women. The biblical view is of equality in diversity.'

If we only had the opening passages of Genesis, it would be clear that God created men and women to be equal and to care for and manage His creation together, without the prescription of roles. The outworking of that commission would be something that was based on the individual personalities and gifts of the people concerned and that they would find ways of working out their roles based on their maleness and femaleness.

We may say that in life today most men are stronger than most women, but there is generally a closing of that gap with some overlap. It would be ignorant to see such things in terms of superiority or inferiority as far as gender is concerned. Even in the New Testament for example Paul's definition of Phoebe in Romans 16 is 'minister'. This is a masculine word denoting her office and not her sex. The word elder is also conveyed in masculine terms as an office. At the end of the Romans 16 is a list of people, which is one third female. Paul says 'I urge you brothers to submit to such as these....'.

The cultural atmosphere of insecurity and fear of women has over the years is built into many Bible translators and commentators preconceptions and into the way they have handled the Bible. This has reinforced the problems from a theological point of view. We cannot altogether avoid imbibing cultural atmosphere such as prejudices, preconceptions and fears from the wider community as they infiltrate the Church. As a result many women feel deprived not being male. These issues need addressing personally and within the community.

Women are not in any way inferior to men, in fact you could argue a good case for the opposite. Any group of downtrodden people has to emerge with a hidden kind of strength. This is true of many racial groups and also of many women today. In creation God made woman from and for man. In redemption, 'in the Lord' this balance is redressed and woman is not now independent of man, nor man of woman. There is complete interdependence. This is the heart of God, male and female together.

CHAPTER ELEVEN

Murdering a Mother?

HOW WE VIEW AND treat our mothers affects many aspects of our lives. Many of us as children felt defenceless against wrong parenting and our reactions today reflect this. Men as well as women often withdraw from that which threatens them. An undue emphasis placed on the technical and rational, with a rejection of the 'feeling' side of things, is often rooted in a neurotic dread of receiving protection and tenderness and is often associated with an original maternal conflict. A cold rationalist attitude can, therefore, be armour against feeling defenceless.

It has been said that men who tend to be initiators tend to overtly 'murder' their mothers in their aggression towards their wives, while women respond covertly and 'murder' their mothers in their inner selves and die as persons. Another way of looking at this is in the issue of the games that are played. Girls subordinate the game they play to the continuation of relationships, while boys continue the game in disharmony! Watch any competitive game at school.

Perhaps it is in the recognition of one's own position with its given history that help is forthcoming. Within the church, however, structures and politics have been formed and need addressing. Have we yet begun to understand first base issues in this matter?

Charles Whitehead begins for us by reflecting on his history. 'When my father returned permanently from the Second World War, life for me changed completely. We left my grandparents and became a family unit, where my father was both kind and loving as well as being an authority figure, which the army had trained him to be. Love was to some extent conditional on right behaviour, or at least that is how I saw it.

'My mother was a strong woman and I grew up believing both mums and dads were equally strong. Mother had made all the decisions in my early childhood in my father's absence. When he returned they seemed to make them jointly. In some areas he would have more to say, for example, in questions of sport. It was he who taught me tennis and golf and took me to watch rugby. My mother only organised tennis lessons for me!

'All this helped me to see women as partners

and equals, but with different areas of responsibility. I cannot identify with having been controlled by these relationships. I see the relationship between men and women as fairly balanced, and I look for that myself, neither wanting to be in control, nor wanting to be controlled. Men and women are different but they are complementary to one another. I like the word "partnership".'

R. T. Kendall is not aware of his parent's effect on him, but realises that they must have affected his outlook. 'I have a strong father and my mother was the classic submissive wife who was sweet and meek. She died when I was seventeen years old. My father remarried and my step-mother was somewhat different.'

Roger Forster sees that men in their aggression towards their wives are trying to get away from the dominance of the female. 'Men need to recognise that it is at least a possibility that there is within them some hatred towards women, or at least to acknowledge it in history, even if not in themselves if they have had a really good upbringing. It dismays me that many men cannot see in history that women have been abysmally exploited.

'We are able to see the racial issues far more clearly today, yet we are still unable to see the female issue. A woman is more passive on the sexual side, needing care and love to be awakened and has, as a result, been more vulnerable. As she is the physically weaker vessel man has made use of her.

'I am not aware of having been controlled by my father or mother. As a child, I found at times that my father would understand me far better when there was an issue and I wanted to get my mother off my back so to speak. He was only angry very occasionally, and even when I did things wrong he understood me and he rarely lost his temper. This helped me to identify with him, and become detached from my mother.'

Dave Tomlinson shares from his history. 'My mother was remarkable. She became the provider in the house, taking responsiblity for our physical well-being. She never became a controlling person and she was constantly laying her life down. I have great admiration for her and can say little that is negative about her. Her effect on me minimised the effect that the wider community's antagonism towards females fed into me.

'My father, although not questioning the traditional concept of roles, had to be a weaker dependent person, being disabled. This must have helped to lay the ground in me, in practical terms, to progress beyond the stereotypes. All my father's dependency never minimised or diminished, in my eyes, the man within him. This has helped me to see that you do not judge people by outward appearance.'

Gerald Coates' mother died twenty years ago, so he has neither the benefits nor the pressures of that relationship. 'I am fairly honest and if I felt that my relationship with one of my parents was controlling me, I would probably share and ask the advice of others that I trust.'

How we deal with power is a key issue in our lives. If we have a problem historically, culturally or in both areas, we need help to move forward to a better place. In being counselled we can find some answers. In seeing good role models in the Church we can move on towards maturity.

David Alton feels that there is not a person in this world who has not been affected by their relationship with their father and their mother. 'I am very grateful for the good things my parents have given me, especially for the influence of my mother. I am also grateful for the help of the nuns who taught me in developing my faith.

'When people try to dominate or indoctrinate you, you ultimately reject them. This was never the case with my mother or my teachers. Even worse is the abuse some children suffer at the hands of their own parents. Recently I read in the press that a new helpline had been established for people who have been abused by women. In a short space of time, 150 calls had been made asking for support.'

Tony Higton is aware of being an insecure child with a fearful father which made him unduly influenced by women. 'I became rather dependent. God dealt with that many years ago.'

John Noble's father died when he was sixteen and he does not recollect having been controlled by his mother, mother-in-law or wife. He continues, 'I was a fighter from the start, which was very nearly my downfall. I loved the women in my life, but in my efforts to control rather than be controlled, I almost destroyed all hope of loving relationships. I don't think I feared being controlled so much as finding myself frustrated to the point of exasperation, because I could not control and at the same time foster love.

'Perhaps, had I learned the secret of affection and romance I might have succeeded, but that would have produced a different kind of snare. That would have meant I would have been a

Casanova as opposed to a Hitler. It has been
the coming of the Holy Spirit into my life which
has increasingly brought peace between me
and the women around me. He has taught me
how to relate to them and value them.'

Joel Edwards' mother was not a controlling
woman, but rather oversupervisory when he
was a child. He explains, 'I have seen in my life
an attempt to break away from all that this
means. An adolescent boy does not want his
mother or his father to be overbearing or to
oversupervise. I am not aware of having been
controlled by such relationships and later
determining never to be controlled in such a
way again. I am, however, very aware of my lack
of a mother father model and how it fits together. Once again there is a "trial and error" issue
in my own development as a husband and
father.

'My parents had quite a lot of conflict and my
father was not very kind to my mother. This has
made me very sensitive to women and I find it
unimaginably evil that a man should hit a
woman. My history has, therefore, affected how
I relate to women. Socially, within my marriage
I consciously avoid any repetition of that kind
of conduct. This more than anything else has
influenced my response to women in general.'

Phil Mohabir concludes, 'I do not honestly think I am aware that any relationships I have had have affected my subsequent relationships with women. I was fortunate in that my mother set a very good example of a hardworking woman. She loved her children and she as well as my dad was a hero.

'In my mother's life, I saw her vulnerability towards men in society and this made me aware that women can be very dominated. I saw the unfairness and injustice of male domination over women. I also need to say that I have seen in life female domination and manipulation of men, which is equally wrong.'

In Ibsen's *Hedda Gabler* we are shown the dread emanating from the buried image of the threatening mother coming to the surface. This woman cannot love; all she can do is compete. She can never be lost in another. She, therefore needs passive and weak men. But a woman needs to learn just as a man does that such power is empty. The battle of the sexes can be derived from a perceived or real threat to a man's masculine identity as he attempts to individuate from his mother.

We often withdraw from power which threatens to overshadow our own. Men are no exception to this. Christian men need to renounce any resentment against their women and by the grace of God become servants and saviours.

If critical, abusive parents still have effect, those voices must be silenced. Receiving the affirming voice of our heavenly Father can remove the fear received through lack of affirmation by our earthly parents. We become free from wrong control which traps us in failure and we can step out and lead from a position of self-acceptance. Many men today, without God are not fully aware of their need. When men are thus healed, women also find healing and the practical outworking of this is in their redeemed lives together.

CHAPTER TWELVE

Seeing a Woman Through a Wife?

SOME THINGS ARE GROWN and others are made. Love cannot easily be planned or managed. Generally it can only be sown and nurtured. The relationship of a man and a woman together is a reflection of the image of God. For a man looking at a woman there is something mysterious. This reflects the mystery of God. Kierkegaard talked of the intelligence of faith being the capacity to enter into a union of being. Then, seeing woman as the substance, he described the terror of commitment and could not allow himself to be loved.

Other philosophers have stabbed at the issue, from Decartes through Schopernhauer to Sartre. They have had various attitudes, from a hierarchical ladder through to the nausea and hopelessness of having a wife or mother with no heart. Others see man's restlessness as fleeing from and running after something; going for it, but in effect being pushed. The only way out of this restlessness is said to be through a death occurring!

Married men can be said to have overcome this restlessness, but at what cost? Have they forfeited their clear attitudes towards women? Has the marital link altered philosophies? Has it opened up new vistas? How does being married affect our attitudes to the opposite sex?

Dave Bilbrough knows that his attitude to his wife has affected his attitude to other women and also to women in leadership. 'I went to a boys' school and was somewhat conditioned. Being married to Pat has shown me that she can function better in certain areas than I can. This leads me to believe that other women can also function better. Pat also has a good leadership gift, therefore I am positive about women in leadership in the Church. At a meeting recently I was singing prophetically and it opened up a door for Pat to come in and be much more specific in applying the word.'

Steve Chalke continues by sharing about his marriage. 'Our biggest problem has always been learning to understand that we are different personalities with different needs. I am an extrovert and constantly enjoy company. My wife needs time alone. I make decisions quickly; Cornie often wants to wait, without knowing why. I am learning to go more with her intuition. This means that I also listen to other people's intuitive statements more.

'I am a radical; Cornie is much more conservative (not politically). I used to think we needed more revolutionaries in the Church. From my marriage I have learnt that conservatives are very important. We need them to ask the questions that slow us down, making us ponder our logic. Here in Oasis our executive director is a conservative, compassionate and sensitive person. I do not feel frustrated with him. If he left Oasis, it would be an awful day. So my attitude to my wife has had an influence on my attitude to people in general, not just towards women in particular.

'I do not perceive all women to be in quiet unassuming roles like Cornie. Our four children are interesting. Emily is an outgoing extrovert. Daniel is quieter and sensitive. Abigail is outgoing. Joshua, the youngest, again, is a quiet child. We might have expected the boys to be extrovert and the girls introvert, if they took after us personally!

'On the issue of women in leadership, much revolves around the fact that men have had more opportunities than women. To speak to six thousand people in a big top, women must be given the opportunity to speak many times in other smaller places. Of all the men who are given such opportunities, only a handful are able to function at that level.'

Joel Edwards' wife Carol is a very laid back person. She passionately hates the limelight. The stereotype of the pastor's wife who does many upfront things is unnatural to her. This has impacted on Joel's attitude to women in ministry and he has formed the opinion that people should not be pushed into stereotypes.

'Carol is not an upfront leader, but a woman of influence. She can make an impression on people; she loves children and could stay with them all day. She has a gift of helps and does not care if you walk past her without realising she is the pastor's wife. In fact she relishes that when it happens! Because Carol is an unconventional pastor's wife, I have been liberated to accept women in ministry wherever God has happened to put them, without the usual stereotyping.

'We need to find out where people are at in their own development and where they perceive themselves to be. We then need to challenge, encourage and provoke them to be the best they can be for God. We need to extend this to the whole family of relationships within the Church, asking what is each person's gifting. Another question might be "Is she the right person to be in this position?" '

John Noble shares from the scriptures. 'This issue surely can be summed up in the words of Ephesians 5:25 "Husbands love your wives, as Christ loves the church and gave himself for her." No husband can properly love his wife until he dies to his own selfish ambitions. I well remember

the day when I said to Christine, when we were
going through a really difficult time together, "I'll
lay down my ministry to get our problems sorted
out!" At first she thought that this was emotional
blackmail. It was not. I was in deadly earnest. My
relationship with her was more important to me
than my ministry.

'I believe that if a man has truly dealt with personal and vested interests in his life most women
know it and feel secure. Such women will not be
taken advantage of, they will not be used or
abused and, in this atmosphere of trust they will
thrive and give of their very best. In these circumstances women begin to take up and utilise their
leadership qualities. However, this may sound
condescending as history is littered with women
who did not wait for men to change, but broke into
the male domain to do what God had destined for
them anyway.'

Charles Whitehead's relationship with Sue his
wife has positively affected his attitude to women
in general and also women in leadership. He continues, 'Our marriage is very much a partnership.
When we came through to faith in the Lord and
began to function in a church setting, we both had
certain gifts which were recognised. Because we
tended to function in a high Anglican church or a
Catholic context, we have always found ourselves
in positions of responsibility and leadership.

'In my business life, I have no problem with women in positions of authority in the companies that I am involved with, because I recognise that they have the gifts for the job. For example, in Sweden, we have a woman who is head of our technical and research division, which she does extremely efficiently. I am also aware that colleagues can be incredibly patronising, making comments that would never be made to a male colleague.

'My attitude in this respect comes from several sources. Parental input would cover perhaps 40 per cent of my attitude. My experience with my wife Sue, might, playing to my parenting, would be just 20 per cent, and my relationship with God and my conviction as to how things should be in a Christian family and church would comprise the other 40 per cent. This 40 per cent would be the thought-out position and the other 60 per cent is experience, but I was not finally in this position until I had come to real faith.'

Some wives are gifted with a powerful ministry, which can be threatening to their partner and his security. This needs to be worked through. It is often a team situation which helps in such situations.

Many ministers' wives are very frustrated. They are often considered only as an 'also ran' and need encouragement to be liberated. They must become who they are meant to be in relation to their personal gifting, otherwise they are less than persons.

R. T. Kendall says that it is possible that his attitude to his wife has influenced his attitude towards women and to women in leadership, but he has not analysed it enough to know in what way. 'Some of my best friends have been interviewed for this book and you can predict what their view will be, because their wives have as high a profile as they do. My wife leads the ladies' meetings and has probably the highest profile of any woman in the church here, I can safely say that she is greatly loved.'

Dave Tomlinson feels that marriage is the deepest relationship in life and must have a profound effect upon anyone. 'As I have seen the ways in which I have abused my wife (not physically but in other ways) and limited her potential in the past, over the years I can see too how I have done this with my sisters in the Church in general. Facing the issue of my domination has really helped me to repent in practical terms and to long to see a fuller expression of the potential within women.

'My wife has had to live with me and be married to someone who is in leadership in the Church in an up-front public kind of way. This is not the direction that her life is taking at the moment. She has had to find her own way forward, which has been quite difficult in view of other people's expectations. But in doing this she has helped me to reform my own views of leadership in general, by expanding in my mind the way that leadership is expressed. Some of the more obvious, very vital and more personal sides of leadership have been highlighted for me, such as dealing with individuals. Pat has liberated me from prejudice and has helped me rethink what leadership is all about!'

Gerald Coates shares how in early marriage he took Anona for granted as she fulfilled certain roles and expectations. 'Later I realised that God does not owe us anything and others owe us nothing. Yet God has made a commitment to us, so Anona and I made a commitment to each other, which brings responsibility to affirm, encourage and express gratitude. As time passed, I have taken Anona less and less for granted.

'Men often take genuine interest in other men but do not take a great deal of interest in women, even when the woman is the wife of a man who is well known. I often have letters from women thanking me for taking the time to speak to them and their children as well as to their husband! I realise that I have a small gift of sensitivity which is not normal to most men, who will often talk to the husband and ignore the wife. Single girls are ignored even more. This is not stated, and men do not generally know that they are doing this as it is part of their mind-set.

'Men are not good at giving dignity and respect to women. It is partly the result of task orientation and partly a hangover from the past, when women were not thought to be good at discussion, dialogue and debate with a high level of interest, which is completely untrue. Some of the most boring people I know are men!

'From my limited pastoral experience, I have found that most men who have a problem with women have it reflected in their relationship with their wives and in the way they treat them. The way some Christian leaders speak to their wives is nothing short of appalling and you would not treat anyone else in that way!'

For **Phil Mohabir** it is through his wife that he has learned that he needs to appreciate women. 'If properly valued they are not a threat at all. During our first year of marriage, we were already in a team as full-time Christian workers. My wife is perceptive. She saw things in my co-worker that were not right! I was so blind to it that I argued with her. I even tried to say to her that I thought that she had a problem with this person. She then just left it and kept praying until my own eyes were opened. I had to come back to her and tell her that she was right and that I needed to listen to her a lot more. From that day on, I've learned that it pays to listen to your wife.

'It is incidents like this that have helped me appreciate and value the opinions of the sisters in the Church. They are not always right, but I have learned to respect them enough to listen to them and not rule them out of court just because they are women. I have also learned through my wife, to appreciate that women bring into leadership a focus, a whole spectrum of views, and a fresh aspect in given situations that will escape a man. After 35 years of marriage we are still learning to be good partners!'

David Alton concludes. 'My wife is very different from my mother in many ways. She was an officer serving at NATO High Command in Naples. She resigned her commission and went to work with mentally handicapped adults with Leonard Cheshire. We met through politics, when I set up the prayer breakfast at a Liberal Conference. When I introduced my Private Members Bill, Lizzie was chair of the Alliance for Life Group and, therefore, a great support. She had held several leadership positions before we were married, and I would applaud more women who, like her, aspire to leadership today.

'Looking back over my political life during the past 15 years, there has been one woman for whom I worked harder than any other candidate in any other by-election. That was Shirley Williams. I had very much hoped to see her emerge as the leader of the then Liberal/SDP Alliance. Simultaneously, the country was run at that time by a woman whose qualities I recognise but do not particularly admire. Being harder or harsher than other people is not a particularly good attribute in either men or women. The idea that you shout louder, rather than seeking partnerships and co-operation is anathema to me. To me saying that words like compassion are weak words is pathetic.'

If you are married to a terrific woman, that makes you think that women can function at any level. If you are in a team with a woman of calibre, then the men have to acknowledge and accommodate such a woman, even if their wives are not like that. If, however, you have not got the right church conditions, you might invent your theology on the basis of your negative experience. If you only ever met women who were hopeless in leadership, it would presumably also affect your thinking.

The drama of history relating man to woman somehow mysteriously links the drama of the Holy Spirit with the figure of woman. The enemy will do everything to work against this; indeed he has done, since he knew it was the seed of woman that would bring forth Christ.

We have suppression of woman at one extreme and the Playboy image at the other. Neither attitude makes men more masculine. Suppression of women comes from a wrong dominance and pornography makes men yield to women. In thus losing the initiative man also loses some of his masculinity, going out to conquer women instead of himself.

Our concepts need radical restructuring. A man yielding to God can trust Him for his future mate. We do not live in an instant world and yet the urgency of sexual desire makes waiting a nonsensical 'suffering' in our culture. A man who knows, as King David did, that sexual sin is a sin primarily against God and not woman (because man and woman together make up the image of God), will prize sexual fidelity at all cost. His attitude towards women will thus be tempered by his attitude towards his wife, through whom in a measure he will view others. His view will be the clearer and he will want to see development of all gifts and abilities to the full.

Commitment for life is a terror which has to be faced. Any person considering marriage has some level of anxiety. Any Christian coming to the scriptures from any background, either chauvinistic or a more equable one, has to ask the related questions in order to gain a theology which can be effective in practice. These gentlemen are aware that their attitudes here have a marked effect on how they relate to women in general and to women in leadership in particular.

MEN IN RELATIONSHIP TO WOMEN IN THE CHURCH

CHAPTER THIRTEEN

Only Male Authority?

THE ISSUE OF MEN assuming authority has been with us since the Fall. Men, having looked at women, continue to blame them for their difficulties in life and try to resolve the issue by placing them in subservience, although this is often unconscious. With some exceptions, whole cultures have had their various ways of keeping women in their place.

Many men follow the maxim 'I did it my way', even within the Church. They attempt to distance themselves from the feminine, conform to the old stereotype of a masculine male in isolation, assuming a role which seems virtuous, and always assuming authority. How can we address this question, other than by asking our male friends to express their feelings and thoughts and make space for women? I let them speak!

Gerald begins for us. 'Yes, women are equipped to handle authority and rule. We see it in business, commerce, industry and politics. It is absurd to suggest that they do not have the same degree of authority as men. Some men are ill equipped emotionally and intellectually to give any leadership at all.

'As a male leader, I do assume authority more because of my role as director of both Pioneer Trust and Pioneer Team rather than because of my attitude to women. It does not mean I have the loudest voice or the greatest say. It may mean that I give a lot more space to a woman like Christine Noble who may not be heard, and if I do not do that no one else will, because it is my role as the leader to do so.

'My leadership role varies from chairperson to director. When I am chairing the Team, I am not pushing through lots of issues. I am facilitating my team to dialogue and each person is to be heard. As the director I am making decisions which I try to make within fellowship and dialogue, so that if things do go wrong, the finger cannot be pointed at me but is rather pointed at us.'

Joel Edwards explains his own position. 'By virtue of having authority in the Church, I have to assume authority. If God calls someone to have authority, He equips them to do it, whether male or female. Some of the women in leadership that I have come across are certainly not ill-equipped to handle authority. So I seek to recognise the call of God in someone's life and release it. Sometimes people do have emotional quirks and we have to work through things.'

Steve Chalke feels that women are equipped to assume authority. He explains, 'Leadership is about team. Women fit into team just as well as men. In our local church our most emotionally stable leader is a woman. She is the one who can be relied on always to be there and not be thrown by feelings and circumstances. She is much more consistent than any of the men.'

David Alton feels that anyone who speaks longer than five minutes with Mother Teresa of Calcutta, will recognise that women are quite capable of assuming authority and leadership. 'I was privileged to show her around London and arrange for her to see the Prime Minister with whom she raised the issues of homelessness and abortion. She did not need titles or trappings. She had clear authority because of who she is and what she has done in her life. Even Prime Ministers and Presidents have an open door for someone of her calibre.

'In our local church, I see the work done by women. They often take on difficult tasks and do much of the visiting and organising. Without them the parish would fall apart.'

Tony Higton continues, 'Clearly some women are

emotionally equipped to handle authority and rule, while others are not. However, for me this is not the primary consideration. It is rather whether God allows that authority and rule to be handled by a woman. There are biblical and historical exceptions (for example, within the missionary movement).

'God is a realist. He can give a gift to a particular person just once in a lifetime, to meet a specific situation. I do not have a rigid view of the gifts of the Spirit, nor do I have a problem with God making exceptions on the issue of women in overall leadership. After all, Deborah led Israel for a period of time in the Old Testament. The exceptions are an embarrassment if you take a really hard line, which I do not.'

Some women do handle certain situations far better than men do. In some situations a wife can be far more mature and effective whereas the husband will become either quiet or overstrong. She is well able to lead yet in other situations she lets him lead. If we can only learn what each other's strengths and weaknesses are, we can complement and not threaten one another.

History too helps us to see the other perspective. In Celtic and Saxon society, women's traditional role was not necessarily inferior. Tacitus remarks on the strange fact that among the Germanic tribes 'Their men knew that in woman there was a certain uncanny and prophetic sense, they neither scorned to consult them nor slighted their answer.' The Picts expected women to play their part in the management of affairs, short of fighting. Their succession came through the female line. Three chief kingdoms of pre-conquest England were christianised by the influence of three devout Queens. These were Bertha of Kent, Ethelburga, who married Edwin of Northambria and her granddaughter, who married the king of Mercia.

Many in the Church have argued that because Adam was created first before Eve, he should have predominance and lead, yet they fail to see that the whole animal kingdom was created *before* Adam, therefore, logically Eve should be and in fact was the crown and perfection of the creative act, at least Adam thought so! Often such thinkers go on to interpret Paul's teachings with their own prejudices, making them more restrictive than he ever intended.

Dave Tomlinson does not feel there is intrinsically anything in women that makes them less able than men to lead. He explains, 'Women are not unable to take up any position of authority or leadership in the Church. What they have to overcome is that historically they have not had the opportunity to do so. In the book of Timothy, Paul says that women must be allowed to learn, and that meant they must be free to make all the mistakes and go through all the processes that men have done. So today, women must be given the right, the opportunity and the space to make mistakes, to learn and develop in the way that men do.

'It is very sad when a woman has been given space and makes mistakes when a man is on hand to say that this has happened because she is a woman! Women are under pressure to do the job and do it *better* than men, which is unfair. We must find women who can fill the slot of preaching and teaching before very large numbers of people. It is inevitably going to be hard to find those women at the moment, because few have had the opportunity to develop those skills. We are in an overlap situation and the more women are given opportunities, the more they will develop.'

Dave Bilbrough assumes authority within his area of gift in given situations. He explains, 'Within certain parameters and in various areas women are also obviously equipped to handle authority and rule. At times a man can be a little more robust at handling things with the implications of what he feels. I fear for a woman out on her own and see "team" as the key to all our needs in these areas.'

Roger Forster has said many times that it is

absolutely scandalous that women who pioneer in missionary work and face all the dangers there, are not then allowed to come back and address the Church. 'In any group there are times when I would expect Faith to assume authority because I know she has the leadership in that area. It is also true with others in our team, male or female. You can only assume the authority that you know you have from God, which is that which has been recognised and stated. You then have boundaries and can function well. The assuming of authority is unnecessary when you know what each person's forte is.'

John Noble feels that the words 'Handle authority and rule' sound male-inspired. 'If we see all leadership in the Church as a service designed to "equip the saints for the work of ministry", then our understanding of authority changes. Jesus did not come to earth to "handle authority and rule"; He came to serve, to seek and save that which was lost. I believe that He did not place final authority in the hands of men, even apostles, but in the gathered church. In Matthew 18 He said that if we cannot resolve a problem we must "take it to the church", not to the men or even to the male leaders!

'Traditionally men have said "a woman must not have governmental authority", although what that is I have yet to understand. Usually it means deciding what colour the vestry curtains will be or how much to spend on a new communion table, which are luxuries that the early church could not afford. However, in practice what they really meant was "as long as you do not do it here" or "providing we cannot see you leading, it is OK!" '

'Thus women for the most part went to the far corners of the globe, often the most dangerous places on earth, to fulfil their calling in God. If they failed and came home dejected and defeated, we said that they "should never have gone" and "that is what happens to women when they lead". If they succeeded, as many did, we said "they are the exception which proves the rule!" This is a typical catch-22 situation.

'Of course, women can "handle authority and rule" if the Holy Spirit anoints them to do so. It has been proved over and over again. Look at Mother Teresa and Jackie Pullinger for starters. If fallen woman is not emotionally equipped to do it then neither is fallen man! That's why Jesus restored both men and women to do the job together as God originally intended.'

R. T. Kendall concludes. 'Whether a woman is emotionally equipped to handle authority and rule, depends on the woman concerned at the time. There are the Margaret Thatchers of this world and the Jackie Pullingers. I would not want to label them emotional just because they are female.

Within the Church there has been a feminisation of almost all denominations and only a few men seem comfortable in pastoral roles. The main New Testament metaphors for being a Christian are concerned with the female, new birth, nurturing, caring, being a servant, and even becoming a little child. Men can counter this by turning the Church into a hierarchical institution to distance themselves from their 'feminisation' as Christians and also from women believers. They can become authoritarian with its resultant fruit, while women generally hope for a new day to dawn, particularly when they look at Jesus and His approach to them.

It is true men need to start where they are at, whether it be sport, car, computers or films of wars. An excellent attitude to authority, which came out of military obedience was commended by Jesus when He spoke to the centurian. Church must not feminise male toughness. It must rather see men and woman as people who stress humility and brokenness, which is attractive when presented in a right way.

The right way to present authority is as Jesus did, with a serving heart gifted to lead and anointed to do so. Women are not exempt. Those who are equipped to lead are called to do so. Leadership is a matter of a person's gifts, personality and temperament, whether they are male or female. Someone who has a good self-image, relates well to others, is sensible and knowledgeable will be able to exercise authority which will be accepted and recognised by both men and women.

CHAPTER FOURTEEN

A Social Order and a Church Order for Women?

There is much ambiguity concerning male and female roles and it is mirrored in the ambiguity that we see between domestic and public life. Can a man, who is immoral in his private life, be trusted in public life? Do we have totally different functions in and out of the home? In the church are there different orders with no overlap?

For men to truly appreciate their position today, some would like them all to sit under a woman's leadership gift for a season, as part of a team. They feel that this is a good way for basic issues to be dealt with. However, the issue of social and church order needs to be addressed first, if it has a bearing on the issue.

Some feel that our difficulties come because we fail to recognise a difference between the two. Social order exists in a fallen world until the Kingdom is fully here, and church order is where the future age begins to be visible. Social structures are needed for a rebellious or at the very least an immature society. In Christ, where there is true humility, these structures may well be turned on their heads. For example, a teenager submitted to his parents in family life, could well take some kind of lead over his parents in the Church, this being a matter of attitude and spirituality not position and authority. Leadership is not the goal, but the means to an end, maturity in Christ.

Others feel that home should reflect what church is and church what home is. If we are learning something exciting from God, we want to tell everyone else about it. We bring it into the life of the church which must reflect everyday life, so that we do not have a two-tier dualistic system.

What then is the consensus of opinion concerning this issue of home and church life. Are there leadership gifts for women at all levels? As women move into executive roles in the world, should the Church similarly facilitate such women with gifting.

Joel Edwards begins by saying that he does see two orders, one for the family and one for the Church. 'Within Pentecostalism the concept of female pastor is not strange. Yet within some churches until recently she did not have a status above that of an evangelist. She could not baptise anyone and would have had to get a man to come in and do it.

'Our older denominational churches have a greater problem because they are communities based around the sacrament. The whole priesthood issue takes on an urgency, which is not found in the Nonconformist churches, particularly Pentecostalism, where there is much more spontaneity and body ministry.

'We still have theological anomalies. A woman can be affirmed as a local pastor and be equal with a male local pastor, but she may not go on to be an area supervisor. We still have residual prejudices when looking at the executive level as far as women are concerned, whether they are black or white. Two years ago, in our General Assembly which meets biannually to look at policy, we decreed that women were deemed able to do everything that a man does in ministry. This was a historic decision born out of how we understand the Bible and leadership in terms of the male–female role rather than in terms of sacrament. It will be interesting to see where the next Assembly takes us in terms of the executive level of ministry.

For **David Alton**, the Church is not the same as society at large. 'The Church for example, is not a democracy. Words such as authority and obedience are unfashionable and underused today. We all need to understand them. No one forces us to be members of a church, but when we do become members, we have to accept church authority and obedience to Christ. This may mean that some of the things we want to do, we are unable to do. As far as women in leadership are concerned, there has been a whole battery of illustrious English women effectively challenging the status quo.

'As far as a woman's role at home and its relationship to her role in the Church is concerned, I feel both men and women have roles in both forums. I do not subscribe to the idea that a woman's place is in the home and nowhere else. Nor do I subscribe to the view that men should leave the homemaking role to women. Men have a role there too.

'After the last general election, I felt a real need to be at home doing practical things for a while. This earthed me in my family. I am not an absentee landlord, nor do I wish to be treated as such, although my job does take me away from home two or three days a week. Divorce happens partly because men are not sufficiently rooted in their families and they see "family" as the wife's job. A man who sees family like this is more likely to go off to have an affair.'

For **Dave Bilbrough** these issues come down to areas of gift in the personality concerned. 'Just because someone has a ministry it does not mean that they are a leader. Each of us needs to find roles in which we excel. Many women are good in pastoral situations because they understand relationships, from working things through with children and teenagers at home. Women have seasons in their lives: some things develop for them with time and their husband's co-operation, and can lead to every level of activity, whether local leadership or executive positions.'

Charles Whitehead does not differentiate between church and family life. 'I believe there are executive gifts in both sexes. There are areas within our home life that I know Sue is better at handling, although they relate very directly to what other people might regard as areas in which men ought to be making decisions. This does not bother me, because we share that responsibility. We talk about most things together. Sometimes I may be the one to go and talk to the children, at other times Sue will do it. At other times we will do it together. Our lives are a shared responsibility and I think it is the same in the Church. The issue of headship does not particularly apply in our lives.

'If we came to a point of total disagreement, but had to make a decision, we might come down on either side. Sue might say to me that I needed to be making the decision. If it was an issue of strong concern to her and I was less concerned but knew it was more important for her than me, I would ask her to decide. When we bought a new car, we both test-drove it. I liked it; Sue was not so keen. I said that we should leave that one; she said no, we should have it, because I did five times more driving than she did. We bought it! In the early days of our marriage I made more decisions than Sue, whereas now we make joint decisions, some even without discussion because we just know how the other thinks and feels.

Also if Sue has the capacity to make decisions which would be hard for me to make, then she will make them. We are very much into mutuality.'

Gerald Coates does not differentiate between the two orders at all. 'We must get rid of this distinction between the secular world and the Christian world. The only thing that is truly secular is sin. There is not such a thing as a secular society because God is at work there by His Spirit, either in accordance with people's wishes or against them. Very many people have to draw on the grace of God and the gifts of the

Holy Spirit. This is as true in business as in the Church, and in some cases more so because of the battle they are involved in and the time they have to spend out there.

'The home, like any other setting, needs someone to be on the bottom line. But the bottom line does not have to make all the decisions. It can call others to make decisions. The Bible talks about wives submitting to husbands. It also talks about all of us submitting one to another. This is not the same as obedience. You can obey somebody with clenched teeth without submitting to them, even when you believe they are completely wrong. Submission is an attitude, where you can even say that you would genuinely like to submit to something, but you do have a few problems with it, and you need to dialogue it through.

'It is impossible to believe that what is expected in the big family of God within the church, submitting to one another in the fear of the Lord, is suddenly to be removed when we talk of the nuclear family. If we expect to submit to one another in the Church, young and old, male and female, and if we expect to listen to each other, give each other respect and dignify the process of decision making, we surely must expect the same in what is called the nuclear family (which was never God's idea anyway).

'Dialogue and debate are part of life, irrespective of whether the man is the "bottom line" or "the source". Whatever else this means, it must mean that men should not make decisions on everything. Often the important decisions are made by women anyway, such as where to go on holiday, which schools for the children, how to decorate the house, what to do at Christmas and so on. Women tend to influence these decisions more than men. Practically speaking, it is sheer nonsense to believe the head of the home is the man and that this means he makes all the decisions. He does not, the woman does, and this shows there is a gap between people's theology and what actually happens in real life.'

Some men feel happy with a team scenario, where the overall leadership is male, but women are well represented. At this point in time, this is where many churches are at by virtue of the fact that women are only just beginning to lead in given areas. Others are unhappy about a woman being the top executive in the church, just as some women are unhappy about a man being in that position. The issue then becomes one of isolation versus team.

Phil Mohabir says that he sees in the Church

an order for government, gifts and ministries which is very different from the general social order. 'Because we mix up the two we tend to take the whole thing to one extreme or the other. I have no problem with a lady I know who is the executive director of a missionary society. I have no problem with women holding positions in leadership as part of a leadership team. I have no problem with ministry at any level, but I am not totally convinced about a woman being the top executive in the church. The only problem I have yet to resolve is whether a woman can be an apostle, by which I mean the ministry of laying the foundations of church life.

'All the female pioneering missionaries that I know, after the initial founding stages of the work, found it necessary to bring in brothers. Many were glad when they could totally hand over the leadership. They then either mothered them from the background or supported them. These women were greatly respected and treated with affection.

'Women with unrestrained executive power become harder than any men I know. They can be very authoritarian and legalistic and I have watched with sadness how God used them to bring to birth and maturity a work which has then fallen back into nothing, because they could not work in partnership. This also happens to men who cannot work in partnership. Even Paul in the New Testament was always part of a team and never alone.'

R. T .Kendall takes the view that *kephale* largely means head rather than source. He explains, 'In church therefore, I think that there is no doubt that leadership on the whole is male. It is the unusual woman that makes the exception. This is my view today on the subject, but I would like to withhold final judgement until we reach 1 Corinthians 14 in our Sunday morning studies in a few months' time, when I shall have done an in- depth study on the subject.

'Yes, there are gifts in both men and women to executive level, but they are not necessarily within the Church. A woman like Eva Burrows who headed up the Salvation Army is an exceptional woman. Another such person is someone like Christine Noble who is very intelligent and bright with a great personality. We get on well and she is the sort of person I would enjoy going on holiday with! We would have more fun on holiday than we would if she was on my staff, or, as she would probably say, if I was on her staff! I would love to have someone of her ability on my staff, but it would all depend on what she wanted to do and I would need to know more about that.'

Tony Higton feels that the Bible speaks explicitly about the Church and family and teaches an overall male lead in both. 'We are not at liberty to reject or ignore its teaching. However, it does not give explicit teaching about society, and the role of women's leadership there is therefore open to debate. There have certainly been some very competent women leaders in society.'

Dave Tomlinson does not see this difference between social order and church order. 'I find that this concept of a priestly role in the Church is rooted in an Old Testament concept of priesthood. There are people in all churches, who for years have accepted that women could take strong executive positions in the world, yet not in the Church. This is because when they consider "spiritual" things, church is seen as a male domain. This also relates to our concept of God Himself, thinking of Him as more male than female and therefore needing to be represented by a man rather than a woman in a priestly capacity.

'I believe all this has been superseded by the coming of Christ and the new covenant. I do not see a perpetuated sacred–secular divide of order in the Church and order in the secular community. I rather see life as a whole. If we have gifts and are equipped to do things, then I assume that God intends these things to be expressed.

'The word "leadership" does not appear in the Bible, whereas the word "head" does. I take the view that "head" is to be more understood in terms of source. God created man first, and I do not read any great significance into that, but it seems to give some men an upper hand. Through the Fall and the entrance of sin, something of this fact has been perverted into male domination. The only way I can now interpret my being a "head" is that because of that sinful order which has existed, I have been able to be in a more controlling position than my wife. This means, therefore, that it has been for me to actually lay down my life, as Paul expresses it in Ephesians, and make it possible for Pat to emerge, rather than see something she could grab and take for herself. I understand being a head as being a facilitator rather than a leader or director as such.

'It is a privilege, that many men are able to facilitate in the home and in the marital relationship the full release of their partners and children. I do not see this role as dictatorial at all, nor patronising, but a rather humbling obligation because of the sinful domination that we as men have had in the past.'

Roger Forster concludes for us. 'It is possible that when a woman marries, she might feel that in certain crisis moments if there is no agreement in the home situation, in a council of two then her husband has the right to determine the way forward. This may be the simplest way to order the family, and might be true therefore in the home. However, this simply would not be true in the Church and, therefore, the order in the Church is different to that of the family.

'A woman may well have time and function in the Church, and her husband may not. Leadership gifts can be in men and women in the Church to the highest levels. This has been demonstrated on the mission field and should be seen here as well. Some people misunderstand authority and see it as heavy dominance in the home and in the Church. Authority is, however, service in the way that Jesus acted by washing and cleaning the disciple's dirty feet. This is the way a husband is called to love his wife. In Ephesians 5 the wife is then called to submit to him and let him love her.'

Our gentlemen seem to have various views on this matter. Resolution may come in answer to the next question! However, they do agree that at home just as a woman is a man's helpmate, so a man is a helpmate to woman. A woman who does not accept her womanliness rejects her role of helpmate and a man who does not accept his role will become stressed, producing an inadequate authoritative leadership, losing his real identity which is being himself in relationship to God. The word 'authority' is never used in the New Testament to describe the role of husband nor 'obedience' to describe the role of wife. Men who pretend to be superior to women in their masculinity are divided between the image they try to project and the reality within. Power has to be laid down in order to love.

At Pentecost gigantic steps forward were made by women in the church. They were alongside the men in prayer and when the Holy Spirit poured out gifts, including leadership. They did not have time for silence! Since those days we have regressed into talking about roles. Women have been deprived of productive economic roles, with the supportive adult social network, and have become fulltime wives and mothers. For a baby boy the options are enormous, while a girl can still at times be expected to be just a wife and mother. We therefore divide life into home and public sections. The Church tends to be linked into the public section and we begin to think of two orders. As we consider this further we conclude that it was not meant to be so, in the beginning.

So we can and must work back to the future.

Executive level is not a biblical term. The Church is different to the world. Authority is delegated by God on two counts: firstly character and faithfulness, and secondly gifting and ability. Men and women can be committed and skilled in all kinds of ways and where this is the case, they should be given authority equally to do whatever they are gifted in and called by God to do. If it involves making 'executive' decisions, so be it.

CHAPTER FIFTEEN

A Gender-Related Hierarchy or Mutuality?

THE ISSUE OF GENDER-related hierarchy or mutuality in a team is one of today's primary issues. Many men were raised with an authoritarian father as role model, with the consequent outworking in the next generation of either rebellion or similar modelling. Other men moved into difficulties when a father was not there. The absence of a role model meant the mother was either placed on a pedestal or distanced. The consequential fear or even dread of women is the resulting motivation by which men go on keeping women degraded by low status.

These issues run deep. Men need to be integrated properly into the domestic sphere and thus understand the difficulties of being at home, often alone with small children. Women need to participate in the public world of work in equality to understand the anger a man can feel at having to work. Co-parenting aids these processes and produces a mutuality in the home.

To find mutuality and unity within the Church is another matter. Can such principles be outworked? Are we hopeful that this is a possibility?

John Noble begins for us. 'Under the old covenant the law was given to Moses on Mount Sinai. It was external and exclusive and was written on tablets of stone. The new covenant at Pentecost saw a totally different kind of law imparted as a result of what happened to Jesus at Calvary. The royal law of love, which came by the Holy Spirit, was inclusive and was written on the tablets of our hearts. Peter went to great pains to point out that Joel's prophecy related to the event they were experiencing. This showed that boys and girls, young and old, male and female, could all have a personal relationship with the Holy Spirit.

'All the old barriers were broken down in Christ; it no longer mattered that you were of a different race, or that you were a slave or a young person, a deformed person or a woman. If the Holy Spirit dwelt in you, you could enter with boldness into the presence of God and you could be used by Him. The veil separating us from the throne of God was torn in two once and for all. In real terms this meant that in Christ, class status, racial identity or gender need no longer hinder any one from serving God. Truly, "Where the Spirit is Lord there is liberty'." '

'Jesus began to demonstrate this new freedom even before Pentecost, as He welcomed women into the team which travelled with Him and ministered to Him. Such a thing had not been heard of up to that time and caused great concern to His critics, giving them more ammunition with which to shoot Him down. Soon Paul was to take things further as women became "co-labourers" with him and he gave them authority in the churches. When commending Pheobe to the church at Rome he gave her full authority when he called them to "help her in whatever she required of them". Do not be fooled by the fact that she was called a deacon; every one who functions in the Church is given that title, even angels and Jesus himself.

'Romans 16, with its list of men and women who worked closely with Paul, clearly demonstrates a mixed team and mutuality. I do not see men who hold the view that leadership is male practising these kinds of team relationships which, even if you limit the extent of a women's ministry, were so obviously functioning. I do not have a problem with someone who holds that view. My problem is when they only theorise and fail to show us in practice how to work together in a scriptural way, within the confines of those limitations. Usually they do not work in teams of any kind, even all male teams, and under no circumstances do they use women the way Jesus or Paul did.

'Personally, I do not see hierarchy in church order. I see friends who have been joined together by the Holy Spirit, each with the freedom to exercise the gifts God has given them through mutually submitted relationships. In this context some have been given the primary gift of leadership as apostles or elders, but even that leadership is by example and entreaty not by government and command. It is dependent on recognition and respect not on rights and privileges.'

Roger Forster believes that if you have a team of males and females the problems of ordination can be solved. He explains, 'Somebody may be the first amongst equals, whether male or female. I do not believe that such a person must be male. It has not been the case on the mission field. This whole issue is related to misunderstanding authority in the Church. Authority is responsibility, recognised both by God and by the Church, and it expresses itself in service.'

Phil Mohabir looks for mutuality and team-work and seeks to have women in place in everything he does. **Steve Chalke** sees mutuality in church order and this is the way church works in his experience. He explains, 'For example, tomorrow we have a leadership meeting. Three of our leaders are women, and four are men. There is no distinction. We have two pastors in the church who are a married couple. They work three days with us and two with YWAM. There is no way we see the man as the pastor and the wife as the helper. They are both our pastors, functioning in pastoring roles. We appointed both of them and they both get a salary. There are just as many opportunities for the women as men in our local church.'

Dave Bilbrough looks for mutuality in team work, with representation of all, including youth. This is the only way that he feels we will be able to work effectively in the Church and reach outwards to people in our society.

The issue for some is whether the head of the team is a man. Even with women on the team some are uneasy if the head of the team is other than male. Traditionalists in the Church often cover their fear. They may say that Adam was made first, before Eve, yet if seniority is the basis then older women should teach younger men and women! They may say that Adam was not deceived as was Eve and he is, therefore, a better leader, yet he sinned, knowing fully that he was rebelling. We also need to ask again how it is that most heresies are begun by men?

They may say that women must not teach or lead and will be saved if they submit to their proper functions of child bearing and obedience. So what of the childless woman? They may say that

Paul in the New Testament does not allow wives to take authority over men. Yet the word used for authority in that context is *authontein*, which has strong connotations of the self-assertive wrong authority so often used by men against women. How are we to overcome such statements?

In 99 per cent of cases **Tony Higton** looks for mutuality and team-work. 'There will, on rare occasions, be a need for the presiding male elder to take the lead. I do not agree that only equals can be subject to each other as the quotation says. Jesus voluntarily made Himself subject and He was certainly not equal in status to those He subjected Himself to. Neither do I feel that Ephesians 5:21 is just about equals.

'I think a person in leadership can and should submit to others. I practise what I preach in being a member of the Body of Christ. On occasions they have not felt right about something that I thought was right,and I recognised this as God's word to me through them. My presiding role means I *could* decide to go against their advice, but I have never done so.'

Dave Tomlinson looks for mutuality. 'The only thing that stands in the way is prejudice. This blocks our progression forwards as does the lack of time and opportunity. Hopefully, as women develop in the Church, men will see that there is no threat but rather everything to be gained. Churches must move on.

'In the best church situations today, we often have a theory that women can take positions of leadership. We need, if you like, a sex discrimination policy, which actively puts into practice the fact that we are looking for the best person to do a job. We are not looking for tokenism, but for men in planning positions to start thinking of women and have a definite anti-discrimination policy.'

Joel Edwards tries hard to look for mutuality, where the Holy Spirit is indeed sovereign. 'God has asked me to lead people and make room for their gifts. Recently, for example, we have elected to add two women to our diaconate as ex- officio members who have equal rights with the men, although our denomination historically has had all male diaconates.'

Gerald Coates shares his feelings. 'Our God is a God of mutuality. At the end of the age He does not say to us that He has prepared this magnificent throne for us because we have done really well and He is pleased with us, rather He invites us to come and sit in His throne and rule and reign with Him. If Almighty God, who is certainly typified as a man in most of Scripture, yet who is nevertheless Almighty God, creator of heaven and earth, in whom there is no beginning and no end, and no shadow of turning, says "Come and sit in my throne, I am the God of mutuality", how much more must we sinning, limited, inadequate, weak human beings create the same mutuality in relationships in the way that God does? Therefore, between men and women I see mutuality.

'God does not need us. There is no inadequacy or deficiency in the Godhead, but there is in humanity. We do need one another. So mutuality has to be a key. In terms of contextualisation and history we have a male-dominated church. It is inevitable that because women have not been given the same priorities, opportunities and training, that men are thicker on the ground so to speak, in terms of leadership. I hope that we are changing so that there is more mutuality and recognition.'

David Alton concludes for us. 'I do not believe in gender-related hierarchy. There will be some men who are very good leaders. Too many men today are being increasingly placed in a position where they feel they have nothing at all to offer, or sometimes they feel they might be usurping the job which a woman might do. The answer is that the best person should do the job, whether man or woman.

'Ministry implies that we must minister to one another, whether male or female. As a Catholic the differentiation of ministry and priesthood for me does hold a problem, but it is a very minor part of what the Church is about. My wife is rather opposed to the ordination of women to the priesthood, although she strongly supported the ordination of her sister as a deacon, which is a ministering role. Neither of us feel that the ordination of women is a great cause to fight for, as we feel it is destructive for the Church. The question of reconciliation of Anglicans and Catholics is for us much more important.

'If Orthodox and Catholic constitute the majority of the believing church in this world and priests are a problem, then in the interests of ecumenism this is an issue which should be decided together. This need not interfere with Archbishop Carey's properly declared objective of wanting to see a greater role for women in ministry. I feel he has rather confused the Catholic and Orthodox idea of priesthood with the proper Reformed church view of ministry. It is for me, a blurring and it would be much easier to say that the Mass, which is mainly Catholic anyway, is a matter for the Catholics and Orthodox.

'On the other hand reformed Christians are right to talk about the role of a minister. There is enormous scope for agreement. Inside the Catholic Church, huge numbers of women are becoming eucharistic ministers and in due course will be deacons as well. The Roman Catholic priest is no longer a solitary male; he is often flanked by women who are in a leadership role, distributing communion and taking it to the sick. Women are called and designated as having gifts and ministries personally chosen and then affirmed by the Church. This is not so far away from the Reformed church view of ministry. To have arguments about the role of priests and the priesthood by the creation of priestesses is, to me, a highjacking of the debate by militant people working for their own ends. It does not enhance the cause of women, but rather damages it in other areas.

'I have no problem with someone like Eva Burrows heading up the Salvation Army, nor women inside the Catholic Church working and leading in ministry. None of those I know are saying they also wish to become priests. Much of the pressure for this has come from outside, creating a further division between Christians. There are already opportunities for women to take on ministry without having to become priests. We are just confusing the two traditions in all this, trying to impose on one tradition something which is alien to it.'

In the formal Catholic setting we only have male bishops and male priests. There is therefore, within that church a gender-related hierarchy. However, below that, running through everything, there is a mutuality of leadership. In the charismatic renewal in the Catholic Church, with the exception of a few of the covenant communities who believe in male headship, there are as many women leaders as men. There may be some men who have difficulty with a woman in leadership, with pastoral responsibilities over them. These issues have to be addressed as specific problems, as well as being seen as a change of system. But they need to be faced and not just glossed over.

The only way to move forward towards the mutuality of Ephesians 5:21, is by the cross. Here we overcome the fear between men and women of who controls whom. God is not speaking strongly about authority and submission, but rather about a new spirit of humility, mutuality and team, where unity is the key prize, 'that the world may know Him'.

MEN AND WOMEN TOGETHER FOR THE KINGDOM

CHAPTER SIXTEEN

Feminisation of the Church or Male Control?

IT IS SAID THAT gender stereotyping coming from an authoritarian father perpetuates a son's insecure masculinity and his later contempt for women. This fills us with horror, yet we do not seem able to alter the status quo. The average north American father spends at most 30 minutes a day parenting. This is mostly chauffering or 'keeping an eye' whilst watching TV.

How can we begin to change our thinking to facilitate change in our thoughts and practices around the gender issue. Are we correct in assuming that men should relinquish overall control? How otherwise can women emerge to take their rightful place?

Charles Whitehead feels that the best way to change men's thinking is to have examples which can be seen to really work. 'Men tend to think things through rationally. If they can be presented with examples where this question of mutual leadership between men and women really works, they will usually see it, become pragmatic about it and begin to change their thinking as a result. It is not so easy to change thinking using biblical texts, because you can also produce other texts and thus enter into a debate. There is no question in my mind that the creation of men and women as equal involves gifting and responsibility thereafter for both.

'I have no problem with both men and women in leadership or in authority, provided they have the gifts for the job. But I respect those who hold another view, because I recognise there are arguments to support it. What upsets me is to see a gifted woman leader, unable to serve in that way because of a narrow and dogmatic view held by others. What a waste!'

Tony Higton says that teaching changes thinking. 'The equality of male and female should be taught from Scripture, as should the fact that gifts and ministries are given to both sexes. We teach consultation, mutual correction and encouragement with the full use of gifts.

'In operating as a theocracy, we encourage women to play their full part in listening to God and sharing their insights. They have a major influence on the Church which is in no way less than that of the men. In fact it is probably greater.

However I do not agree with the statement that men should "relinquish overall control", although I don't like the word "control".'

R. T. Kendall wants to see women released into their gifts and ministries, but would be surprised if the ministry into which they were released were to be one which replaced male leadership. He does not actively work towards changing thinking on this at present.

Phil Mohabir feels that we need some very bold initiatives to be taken. 'The more we write, discuss and debate, the more all we do is postpone action. We need to create models. This will be a demonstration worth more than 100 seminars. We must have a theological base, yet there has to be learning by doing, to facilitate male and female interaction and partnership.'

Dave Tomlinson continues, 'In the Church there is a huge job of teaching to be done. It is not good enough for people to say that they do not have a problem with this issue. We must lay a positive foundation so that this issue does not come to revisit us in the future! We need a positive theology for equality and a clearing away of the rubbish.

'We also have to deal with the prejudices that we have been born with. Awareness which raises and contests the issue is as important as it would be in relation to the issue of race. We must confront racism and sexism consistently without losing our sense of humour and being able to joke about the difficult and painful things in life. Side comments and put-down statements must be confronted and men who are guilty of this, need to be made uncomfortable if they are expressing prejudiced points of view.'

Teaching on this subject is essential. We must allow men to affirm themselves as men who are part of the divine order rather than see them defending their corner at all costs. Wrong attitudes must be relinquished in the service of the Kingdom. Men are not the sum total of the divine order.

Paul in the New Testament encourages women to publicly participate at all levels of church life, provided they are dressed appropriately and modestly, and honour their husbands and take opportunity to learn from others in a quiet and submissive spirit.

Gerald Coates feels that Pioneer needs to model mutuality, as well as women in leadership, giving to both dignity and respect. 'I appreciate there may be stupid or pseudo-spiritual women in leadership just as there are pushy and manipulative women in leadership. However, this is also true of the men and probably a hundred times more true of them. There are men who have been to Bible college but who could not lead anyone out of a paper bag. They have contributed to the massive haemorrhaging of attendance from the male dominated church throughout my entire life.

'We cannot keep holding up stupid, superspiritual, pseudo-spiritual, inadequate, weirdo women as our reason why women should not be in leadership. If we do, we would also have to hold up the same sort of men in the Church, who would find it hard to get a job in regular life, because they are odd, eccentric, without people skills and just plain rude. This is far too shallow an approach for such a serious issue in the Church.

'Through training, fellowship and recognition of anointing and acknowledgement of where God is at work among the men and women, we will reveal what the Church should be like to others. People will then become impressed with what they see working. When you are doing God's will, things do work. So we must model the truth, recognise anointing and leadership skills in women and then give away our power, not because we should give it away to women, but because all leaders should give their power away to other men and women, as their own role changes.'

For **David Alton** women such as Elaine Storkey, have helped and challenged his thinking. Her lectures and talks are quite an interesting way of getting the debate going. She spoke eloquently at a 'Movement for Christian Democracy' weekend on these issues. Opening the debate is the way forward, whilst recognising that there will always be some contradictions and conflicts.

Dave Bilbrough says he finds that a Bible-based doctrine alone can become archaic, while a contemporary society alone mirrors only what is going on in the world's system. He explains, 'We need to be open to change. We need to instil into people that constant change is here to stay. We need to be unprejudiced, allowing the Church not to be locked into one particular model. We need clear Bible-based prophetic teaching, from men and women of vision, which is in harmony with our contemporary society. All these need to go hand in hand.'

Steve Chalke feels that thinking is only ever changed by practice. 'Discipleship happens by doing. Old models are only slowly changed by empowering new ones. We need to model mutuality effectively, with men and women on board. We run 'Inside Out' weekends. We talk to other churches about the needs of the inner city. All the people who teach on these weekends are women. So this is being a model. We are often asked where we get these incredible women from! We reply that they are to be found in most churches and of course they were in other churches before ours, unnoticed!'

John Noble concludes this section. 'It is not just a question of "changing men's thinking", we must all change our thinking. We have all been infected by wrong concepts. Satan has completely duped mankind and has ground this deception into the very warp and weft of our make up. It will take time to purge it out of the Church's system. Women too must face the consequences of this fresh revelation of God's truth. We must work together on all fronts.

'For example, we must develop a new theology which is thoroughly biblical and does not avoid the hard questions. We must take time to train people in teaching and practice. We must encourage women who are willing to step out into ministry on the basis of God's call in their lives. We must continue to love and serve those who disagree with us. Above all we must pray that the Holy Spirit will do what we cannot do in renewing people's hearts and minds.'

Historically men have turned the Church into a hierarchical often bureaucratic, institution. As a result they have distanced themselves from the feminine and intuitive side of their personalities. Jesus teaches men to develop that aspect of character. Most sincere men's thinking can also be changed quickly as they experience a woman's leadership or teaching ability.

Positive role models are also needed today, and need to be seen to work. People's thinking and attitudes change when they see a model that works, which defies contrary theories because it is seen to be viable, biblical and endurable. Objective investigation into such models has great effect in changing mind-sets.

Women too need to change their thinking in order to change practices. Although relationships are important, they cannot be used to shift responsiblity for actions. Nor are they an excuse for not developing talents to the full.

There is an assumption that men should, in a right way, relinquish overall control because it is only when space is made for women that they can find room, without fighting for it. A God-given recognition and practice of what this really means leads us on to the practicalities.

CHAPTER SEVENTEEN

Frustration or Facilitating Fulfilment?

CHANGING PRACTICES IS were the rubber hits the road. If men in control can relinquish as God leads them we will have a church of fulfilled people working together. Women are team players and 'people persons' generally. Their contribution will affect whole communities. The best environment to begin with is one where the whole family reaches out to meet the needs of others. Liberated women produce liberated children.

Dave Tomlinson begins. 'We must have the courage of our convictions and move on to taste and see in this issue. I know numerous churches where the prejudice against women in leadership is dying away, but in reality there are still no women in leadership or you may get the odd one who is the exceptional person. This is just not good enough. Men must begin to work in partnership with women. This will become a more powerful way of breaking down prejudices. Once things are working and operating, there are no more problems than you would expect if you had men in positions of leadership. People will have to admit that the devil is not crawling all over the place, evil has not come upon us and this is actually for everyone's benefit!

'The churches which remain deeply prejudiced will have to be left, and those where headway is being made on a conceptual level will have to put it into practice for progress to occur. We must move forward realistically and not suddenly drop women right in the deep end, where they are almost bound to start sinking.'

John Noble feels that so much depends on each individual church situation as to how we can facilitate change. He shares: 'Some churches and fellowships have already undergone a revolution in relation to women in ministry. Some new churches have grown up never having had much of a problem at all.

'However, it is more usual that we have to go out of our way to create a platform for our women and give extra encouragement to them as they have additional obstacles to overcome when they move out. If a man gets up to preach and doesn't do too well we may dismiss it by saying he had a bad day. If a woman fails in this way she faces the criticism that it happened because she is a woman and the event confirms that she should not have attempted such a thing!

'In these churches we need to be "wise as serpents and gentle as doves". We should not aim beyond our ability to sustain and support our cause. We must not set women up to be knocked down. For example, why not try to get a church to accept women functioning as elders as a first step, especially when the men themselves are probably not functioning properly in that ministry? Let us rather create space and give them titles, if we must, which do not alienate them. Servant leaders or deacons may be appropriate, once they are seen to be functioning successfully and then we can begin to explain what they are actually doing. It is always easier to explain what is taking place rather than what you hope will happen.

'Women should be encouraged to receive training alongside men, where it will quickly be observed that some are more able than their male counterparts. Men should be encouraged to do jobs which are generally left in the women's hands, such as serving refreshments, cleaning, flower arranging, teaching in Sunday school etc. We can begin to break the moulds which have been forced upon us in simple ways. This will open us up, helping us to appreciate one another and see things in one another of which we are completely unaware. It should help to dispel fears in women who hold back in case they are criticised. It will also break the lethargy which paralyses men because they feel that unless a task is "important" it's not worth doing. After all Stephen, the Church's first martyr, started out by waiting on tables.

'When the time is right, we must not be afraid to "bite the bullet" or call a "spade a spade". There will come a moment when we must give women the recognition which they have earned, and fully acknowledge their contribution before the whole church. This is very important as public recognition is both biblical and healthy; it will result in greater security and a further release of ministry.'

David Alton continues, 'When women are being excluded then people need to look at the institutional structures that prevent their voices from being heard. At the Centre for Reconciliation between Protestants and Catholics in Northern Ireland, having resolved the issues as they see them between the two communities, they now find an almost bigger issue which needs resolution first. It is the relationships between men and women. There must be a willingness to be flexible and discuss complaints.'

Dave Bilbrough says that we need practical models. 'We need to be able to look at the platforms and leadership of churches in this country, and see teams of men and women being modelled together. People imbibe what they see. For example, we must not only see male worship leaders.

We must encourage more women worship leaders. One new record came out recently in the United States where the worhip was directed by a woman. This is quite a large step for some over there. Here Spring Harvest and other such Bible weeks are forums where this can be developed.'

Roger Forster sees teamwork as the key to changing practices. He explains, 'The great contribution of Brethrenism to the Church above everything else is team leadership and mutuality of leadership. They however, made it male dominant. If women are allowed in, we have the key for developing women's leadership gifts, which otherwise would not be devloped.

'In setting women forth, standing behind them and backing them up we can create a new order with recognition. Any person is in any position in the church according to the gifts the Holy Spirit has given them. Every church must be training women as well as men. Training is also the key to changing practice. This breaks the circle of women not being involved.'

So training is a key issue as is changing the role models. We must develop models which do not infringe Bible teaching, but rather affirm what it teaches. Recognition, training and releasing are key elements for seeing women moving into leadership.

Steve Chalke continues, 'We change practice by doing it. We can only learn this way. We will sometimes fail and this needs to be recognised. Oasis grew very quickly through delegation. Many try this and say it fails. But the truth is that it does work, but part of the delegation process is failure. In Luke 9:1, Jesus sent out the disciples, two by two, to preach and heal the sick. If you read on in chapter 9 they failed at both pretty convincingly!

However, in Luke 10:1 says that Jesus sent out 72 others, two by two to do the same thing. He did not say it did not work! He said that after all this failure it would work and that he wanted to send out more. Failure is an important part of learning.

'We have swopped passion for professionalism. We do not allow for failure and mistakes in preaching, teaching and healing. The joke is told about some deacons thinking of appointing a woman as their minister. They took her out fishing one day to get to know her. In the middle of a huge lake she said that she had forgotten her handbag. She got out of the boat and walked across the water, got her handbag, walked back and sat down. They thought about what they had just seen and complained that it was just typical of a woman to forget her handbag! Women should not have to be superwomen to function; they must be allowed to fail just like men do and yet still be believed in and encouraged.'

Charles Whitehead feels that changing our practices means bringing women with obvious gifts into leadership, and letting the fruit speak for itself. 'We need to recognise that women bring gifts that men very often do not have, within the areas of understanding and intuition. I remember once sitting on a committee to plan a large social event and we found to our horror that the committee comprised five men. The first thing we did was recognise the problem and acknowledge that we needed women involved. The practical nature of that situation leads people to understand that things should be different. This is hardly an important example, except that it shows how much we lack and lose if men and women are not working together.'

Phil Mohabir actively promotes the sisters in the church, as he has promoted the men. He does this by identifying, recognising, appreciating and giving opportunity to function. He feels that this issue must be faced head on to promote change.

Tony Higton believes that God does not want His gifted people to be frustrated. 'Practically speaking, I would not separate what God has joined together. Therefore couples are used in leadership in our church as much as possible. Where a single person is gifted, we would make a "threesome" with a married couple so that they can lead together. We have no leadership meeting that is closed to women, especially spouses. We must be truly charismatic, practically discerning, respecting and facilitating the gifts and ministries of all men and women.'

Gerald Coates concludes for us, 'At all levels, in whatever area of the Church, whether in our work with children or youth, in teaching, music, worship or evangelism, we need to look at the whole Church and not just a half or a third of the Church. Then we will cease to be an army fighting with one arm tied behind its back, one patch over its eye, hobbling around on one leg. Half our resources are all locked up at the kitchen sink and looking after children at home. Many women are brilliant in leadership, administration and worship. Provided they have earned the right in the same way that we would expect men to do, there is no reason why they cannot begin to function.'

In conclusion most of these men are looking to make space for the many gifted women around their churches. They are looking to recognise, train, facilitate and release. Like Jesus they are not anti-feminine. When He chose twelve male disciples as a symbol of the new order replacing the twelve patriarchs, His attitude remained liberating to women around Him. He did many feminine things; He washed feet, cuddled infants, made breakfast and taught His disciples to wait at table and clear up the left-over food. He spent much time with His women friends, extending the kingdom of God through them and empowering them to preach His resurrection. The Holy Spirit wants all His 'frozen assets' redeemed and at this point in history many in the Church await the outcome.

CHAPTER EIGHTEEN

Male Apartheid or Back to the Future?

IN THE GARDEN OF EDEN, Adam and Eve together had dominion. How this was worked out remains a mystery. Somehow the enemy, along with sin entering in, was able to destroy their harmony and turn them against one another. Man blamed woman, woman feared man. Women have since constantly been the ones who under pressure do all the adjusting. Many times a step has been taken into the world, by a woman. Yet if she has faltered, she has been told that she has the option to return to the home. She is still required to prove herself often without the co-operation of men either at work or at home, where partnership at its best should be friendship.

Even governments who want women to work, retain a social policy which implies that if they do not look after children, the old people and the mentally ill then no one will. Men can more easily evaluate their roles at work whilst women come under severe pressures at times. To back-track and move towards a more godly way, are there steps that we can take to restore what God really intended? Are we able to discover a better way forward than the mish-mash of todays society? Can we indeed go back to the future, by the grace of God?

Roger Forster begins by saying that he feels that there must be a day when we will see men and women in partnership together at all levels of church work. 'If we are to be a witness of the Kingdom to all nations, the only kinds of churches which witness to that Kingdom are those in which there is neither Jew nor Greek, bond nor free and neither male nor female. Such a Church is where male and female relationships are expressed as truly equal. We cannot present men and women as equal if we do not allow women equal opportunities with men to use their gifts in the Church.

'Every revival brings into view the totality of the Kingdom and sometimes one thing or another is highlighted. The Wesley revival highlighted this issue as well as the slavery issue. Wesley had female preachers, who were on a par with men. In the Quaker revival and in the Anabaptist movement the male–female issue was also completely dealt with, with total equality. We are talking here of things which took place in the sixteenth, seventeenth and eighteenth centuries. Hierarchical churches have promoted a wrong image of God's total redemption for men and women, just as national churches have promoted a wrong image in the race issue. The title "Church of England" is objectionable to me, because it says that you can have a church which belongs to a nation, instead of saying that individual people of the nation belong to God or the Church.'

Gerald Coates agrees. 'Yes, we are beginning to take ground back from the enemy. In many of the groups that I know, enormous strides are being made to make room for women. We do have problems such as the availability of women, the skills of women, the whole issue of the security of women, as well as having to relate to the situation of, at best, a male-orientated church and, at worst, a male dominated one. We need an extraordinary sort of woman to do that. If we do not have such women, then there is no way forward, because we cannot just have representation of women, otherwise we would have to apply this criteria to the men! This would obviously not work.

'In our Pioneer network of churches we have women who have been functioning as successfully as the men for years and in some cases much better. This will challenge those who are open to the issue and do not know the way forward. It will also challenge others who are perhaps male chauvinists, or who simply have not thought about it or are afraid of what others might say.

'Our goal is to evangelise the nation, not just produce a holier church. We are called to network the nations with the gospel and then the end will come. So we must release the resources available in the body of Christ for this. This does not mean half the resources in half the body, or relegating women to certain areas of function and not others, because then we will never get the job done. It is all part of our restoration, women coming back into their original intended purpose, which was partnership with God and partnership with men.'

Charles Whitehead too feels positive in answering. 'Yes, I can foresee a day when we will begin to establish this joint rule and I think we are beginning to move towards it. It varies in different traditions. Some of the more evangelical churches seem to find this issue difficult. At the other end of the spectrum amongst the Anglo-Catholic and Roman Catholic churches, the ordained male ministry does make things more complicated. This, however, is being balanced with the kind of teaching now being given which says that (in spite of the reasons why the Roman Catholic Church does not at present ordain women to the priesthood which is a more theological issue than anything else) it does not mean that women should not exercise leadership in the Church. Proof of this is that many women, particularly in religious orders, have very important positions, often heading up major groupings of religious orders.

'Working with our young people in charismatic renewal, we are teaching, preaching, presenting and modelling a balanced leadership according to gifting, irrespective of gender. I am very optimistic, without knowing how we will get to the ordination of women in the Roman Catholic church. I do not feel terribly strongly on the issue at the moment, because we are fighting battles which are more in the area of the role of lay people rather than the ordination of women. We must get this right first.

'Looking at industry where big changes are occurring between men and women, women are now coming into positions of authority within the structures and are becoming part of senior management teams. This is mainly within industries where women tend to have an interest or are gifted in that particular area. We do not see many women managers in the steel industry, for instance, but there are far more women than men managers in the retail industry, with some in the very top positions. We now have a lot of women in the buying area. This makes interesting chemistry, especially when you get the old-fashioned type of salesman who is one of the most chauvinistic creatures alive. He is used to doing his business with a high level of disreputable jokes and he builds relationships on beer, rugby, golf, etc. If he is confronted by a highly professional woman buyer, often he cannot handle it easily. Younger men usually have fewer problems.

'Some companies have very good policies and promote women to all levels. One company I deal with has solved the question of a woman leaving work, and having children and then coming back. They have appointed excellent women particularly into the purchasing side of the company, because when they return after the birth of a child it is much easier to fit back into that side of things, rather than the production or financial side of the business. There are a lot of encouraging signs in business, but I must admit to certain fears about the effects on family life of more and more working mothers.'

Joel Edwards feels that we have a long way to go before we see these things totally worked out. 'Many denominations are considering the gender issue at the present time and I think there will inevitably be changes to be worked through. We need to see leadership reflecting what is happening at the grassroots level. For example, many of our inner city denominational churches are eighty per cent black, but their leadership is all white. Such issues as this need to be faced, just as the gender issue does. No one is either superior or inferior. I have a passion to see mixed race churches and I do foresee a day in church life when we will begin to regain some of this ground. Then there will emerge a mutuality between male and female too.

'I hope this does not come about as a concession which the Church makes to social pressure, to avoid embarrassment and media accusations. I hope rather that it comes about because the Church comes to terms with the theological feasibility of female leadership in the first instance. I also hope that it comes about because we desire to demonstrate the "priesthood of all believers", because men increasingly understand what accountability is and the notions of superiority are put to rest as they become more secure.

'Then the gate will be opened to people who already have the gifting and ministries to emerge. I trust that in all this nothing will have been lost—in the home, divine order or in the Kingdom. Then we will really know what Galatians 3:28 means, theologically and in experience. At present the Church is just beginning to listen to the heart of God on these matters, realising that there is a very painful passage to be negotiated in the days ahead.'

Phil Mohabir says that he is not convinced that God meant a joint rule in the garden of Eden! 'It was a partnership and Adam and Eve were to have dominion and to care for the earth. It concerns me what we do with the environment and with our families. The Church needs to recover something in the heart of God concerning man and woman. What applies to this male and female issue also applies to class, education, status, riches and race. In God's heart there is equality for all people. Let us take back lost ground. Partnership is the way into the future. We must address basic insecurity. Traditions and current role models must be dealt with and corrected. Realistically, it is not being done in the whole church, but we are seeing movement towards it. So let us go for it, in spite of the continuing doctrinal battles, and see more brothers and sisters working together for the glory of God.'

Some do not agree with the argument which underlines this question, and do not see that day coming when we will begin to take back the ground of joint rule. It may come in the eyes of some if that is what they are working for, because they do not have difficulty with the whole concept of partnership. There will remain difficulties for others in these concepts, which will have to be continuously addressed.

David Alton continues, 'Short of the second coming of Christ, we are going to have to continuously grapple and wrestle with these problems. I dispute that slavery has been overcome. At this moment young girls are being sold in northern Brazil and in Thailand as sex-slaves. We are slaves in this country to the idolatry of materialism, to cult pornography, to drugs and to violence.

'The issue of race remains too. Christians are still fighting one another in various parts of the world. We cannot create the Kingdom of God. It will come when God ordains it and not before. However, I do believe that there are steps we can take and there are many more things that we can do. We must never stop striving for justice even though in our imperfect and fallen state we will not see the ultimate successful conclusion to these things, this side of heaven.'

Tony Higton shares his perspective, 'I still believe that the Church should have a male president. For me Galatians 3:27 is about equality of status, not function. There are obvious differences of function between male and female, and in the area of authority there is a difference of function too. The norms of masculinity and feminity predate the Fall. One can argue for the man as normally more of an initiator and the woman as normally more of a responder, and this is from the order of creation not as something resulting from the Fall. Domination, not leadership, came in through the Fall. It seems to me that there was an overall leadership for Adam before the Fall, but it went wrong and became domination with the Fall. Leadership is meant to be liberating, not dominating.'

Steve Chalke looks at a view of the future. 'I hear a lot of triumphalist talk about revival coming. But if I am honest, without pouring scorn, we must have the freedom to ask questions. For example, the Baptist church has been given the goal of planting 2000 churches by the year 2000. Will they plant any? If they did plant them would lots of them be in the wrong places, because 90% of the population is in cities, whereas Baptist churches generally thrive in outer suburbs and provincial towns? If they are aiming to evangelise the nation it will have to be done in the cities and in the rural villages, not just in provincial towns and suburbs. I feel we are still a long way from revival in this country.

'As we plant new churches and evangelise we must also address the issues of women in the Church, ethnic minorities, the working classes, men, youth and non-readers to name but a few. This will force us to be a lot more realistic in the church about our evangelism. This is not defeatist and God will get us there in the end. We have sung that "Now is the time for us to march upon the land" and then we have gone home and watched the telly! It is time for some hard thinking and hard work both men and women together.'

Dave Bilbrough notes that male and female dimly represent the mystery of the Godhead. 'We are at the beginnings of demonstrating partnership. As the next generation rises up, I hope they will take hold of some of these things that godly men and women have pioneered, and with their individuality and diversity express on a much broader canvas the rich tapestry of church life that we long to see fully portrayed.'

John Noble concludes for us, 'It is taught by some that Galations 3:28 should read, "There is no Jew or Greek only Jew, there is no slave or free only free, there is no male or female only male." They tell us that until we receive our new bodies when the fullness of the Kingdom is come, women must relate to God through men. Carry this to its logical conclusion and that would mean that slaves could only relate to God through their masters and Gentiles only through Jews, which is, of course, nonsense. In human and fleshly terms we all know there are still Jews and Greeks, but in Christ and in the realm of the Spirit I am already a Jew because my heart has been circumcised. In the same way a slave has become free in Christ even when he is yet in his chains, and a woman can receive all the promises not only of a male, but of the first-born son and heir.

'The ground is there to be taken—let those of us who see this truth start to live it. It is our privilege to bring the future into today by faith. If by a change of heart I, as a man, can begin to appropriate the promises given to Abraham and his seed now, so too a woman can begin to appropriate the promises given to the male heir, because we are all sons through Christ. None of us should do this in a spirit of militancy and aggression but out of humility and thankfulness. In this way we will make visible what has been invisible and we will demonstrate that faith really is the substance of things hoped for.

'Furthermore, we are not just to take back the ground that Adam and Eve lost, rather we are to go beyond, way beyond this. For we, men and women, are already seated with Christ in the heavenly places. We are destined, not to be ruled by angels as they were in the Garden by Satan, but rather to rule the heavenly powers. Jesus did not tell us to wait patiently until His return before we take authority over demons and evil forces: we are to start right away. What other evidence is there that our message is true, than that it is accompanied by the signs of the future Kingdom invading our earth right now? The gospel of the Kingdom will never be effectively preached to the hundreds of millions of oppressed and abused women of the world unless it is seen to be the good news it really is, which means "you are all one in Christ Jesus!"

'Never before in human history has the need or the opportunity for men and women to be seen working side by side been so great. The time is ripe for Christians to grasp that opportunity and meet that need, but we will only do it if we are convinced of the validity of the message and are filled with the power of the Holy Spirit to accomplish it together.'

The Church is not going to be totally pure in the world and, therefore, there will be sin manifested in numerous ways. Prejudice against women is going to be one area that we will not completely stamp out. Wherever the Holy Spirit is at work, there should be a loosening of hard and fast roles, an affirming of every individual and a liberating of people to be what they are in God. However, with this we need reformation of thinking and theology in order that afterwards things do not go back to where they were.

This issue is like the proverbial toothpaste. We cannot get the toothpaste back into the tube! Things cannot return easily to where they were. This gives us hope. Attitudes have changed, yet old prejudices will be found in pockets. However, the axe has been laid at the root of the tree and women's roles in the Church will be quite different in the future, compared to what we have known in the past.

Our tension is in seeing the future and being in the present. We know the resurrection. We await its final outworking in us. We taste the powers of the age to come, when a new people is coming into being which shall be neither male nor female.

Jesus is our forerunner and at heart both masculine and feminine in His words and actions. He was involved in the creation of Adam and Eve, who together were made in the image of God. He was involved in redeeming both men and women and set alight the relevant perspectives of this for the women around Him. He taught the Church through Paul, not to bring this new found freedom into disrepute, either within the cultural scenario (i.e. head covering) or within the Church, with uneducated women causing confusion in public with their questions. They were to be covered and silent in order to learn. Once they had learned they were a force to be reckoned with as Romans 16 shows us.

All the gifts of the Spirit have been used by women in the scriptures. Church history is full of the many female witnesses. As we move to the close of the twentieth century and the Lord's return, is it any wonder that this ground of freedom is being contested, even by some in the Church, in the way that Jesus was challenged by the religious leaders of his day?

Conclusion

WITHIN THE LAST half-century there has been a marked turnabout in the visibility of women in the world's concerns. Women in politics, in professional life, and in international relations have all made their presence felt. At the other end of the scale many women have been seen to be the world's poor and the world's marginalised. Women struggling to bring up children against all the odds have had their stories heard and reported.

This second scenario is not new. Women throughout history have been discriminated against. In the West this has been as wives and mothers, in education, at work, by the law and by the Church. An answer for some has been to identify with one of the many faces of feminism, whether within the liberal or the radical groupings. The Church's response has been ambiguous. Sometimes feminism has been lambasted and rejected unilaterally. At other times it has been embraced wholeheartedly and indiscriminately.

But there has always been another way forward. Women and men in Christian history, who viewed Jesus's attitude to women as redemptive, began a new dawn. This is in spite of their Church's inability to reject the patriarchal power structures of the day, as Jesus did. They were pioneers and much has been written of them and their work. Today we see a continuation of that new beginning in the biblical feminism active within Christianity. This feminism is not self-absorbed, but it reaches out through and beyond the Church into the community and life in general.

The men interviewed in this book are for the most part favourably inclined and theologically persuaded in the matter of biblical Christian feminism. For it embraces liberation for both women and men, and that liberation engages so much of life, the emotional as well as the political. Men are increasingly owning their feelings, not wanting power and control, but rather the opposite, which is love. They are working amongst women who do not want power either, but rather to be part of the team. As a result, both are finding in a new way the grace and blessing of God.

I know many of these men and respect their work. I look forward to the future and to hearing about the good things that they and their teams are doing. For as we work together in mutuality, we can see the outworking of justice and cooperation. When we give back our leadership to the grace of God we know the humility which marks out true Christian service. It is together, in faith and in the power of the Holy Spirit, that the future of our Church and of our witness lies.

Elaine Storkey

Bibliography

Dalby, Gordon *Healing the Masculine Soul*, Word UK, 1989

Dobson, Ted *Healing the Tear in the Masculine Soul*, SCRC Vision, 1985

Ehrenberg, Margaret *Women In Pre-History*, British Museum Publication, 1989

Gaebelein Hull, Gretchen, *Equal to Serve*, Scripture Union, 1989

Korda, Michael, *Male Chauvinism*, Berkley Publishing Corporation, New York, 1972

Le Sourd, Leonard, *Strong Men, Weak Men*, Hodder and Stoughton, 1990

Martin, Joan *The Ladies Aren't For Silence*, Word U.K., 1991

McCloughry, Roy, *Men and Masculinity*, Hodder and Stoughton, 1992

Moore, Katherine, *She For God*, Allison and Busby, 1978

Noble, Christine, *What in the World is God Saying About Women?* Kingsway, 1990

Pawson, David, *Leadership is Male* Highland Books, 1988

Payne, Leanne, *Crisis in Masculinity* Crossway Books, Westchester, Illinois, 1985

Stern, Karl, *Flight From Women* Allen and Unwin, 1966

Van Leeuwen, Mary Steward *Gender and Grace* I.V.P., 1990

Storkey, Elaine *What's Right With Feminism?* Third Way Books, 1985

Storr, Anthony *The Integrity of the Personality* Penguin Books, 1960